Steve's Chronicles

Book 1: Steve in the New Nether

By

Blaze Block

PUBLISHED BY:
Blaze Block
Copyright © 2021

TABLE OF CONTENTS

Chapter 1: Green Fields 5

Chapter 2: The Adventure Begins 10

Chapter 3: Crafting 14

Chapter 4: Warning 17

Chapter 5: Mobs and Tree 24

Chapter 6: Railroad 29

Chapter 7: Convoy Attack 47

Chapter 8: Wastelands & Adventurers 53

Chapter 9: Obsidian Battlements 66

Chapter 10: War Brewing 79

Chapter 11: A Friend 95

Chapter 12: The Battle 99

Chapter 13: The Dark One 114

PLEASE LEAVE A REVIEW 126

Chapter 1: Green Fields

The dogs were running around outside as Steve opened the oak door. His diamond armor almost seemed to glow from the light of the sun as he walked forth from his home.

The three-story structure was dotted with windows and had a balcony wrapping around the uppermost floor. The mix of wood, stone, and iron hosted torches that burned comfortably between every window.

He would replace them before the sun set.

The crops to his right, by the water, were growing well. There were fields of carrots, potatoes, and wheat. Beyond, a villager from across the bay, whom he'd hired as a cartographer, was working at his station. At times, he looked up to see the stables across the cobblestone road from.

Staggering hills rose to the north, hulking green things with red speckles here and there. A few gulls were circling above the beach, while crows flew above the trees.

Steve began walking to his little harbor, that had just two stone piers.

Two rowboats sat anchored there.

As he reached the dock, about to board one of the boats, he caught sight of another boat rowing towards him.

"Trader," he muttered.

This trader had been bothering him every day now.

His camels always kicked him, and the trader only offered things Steve already had – chests of gold, diamonds, end eyes, and redstone.

"Go away!" He shouted at the purple-cloaked trader as he approached. "I've told you before! Go away!"

The trader didn't seem to respond at first, but then Steve thought he heard his muttering as he stopped rowing beside the other pier.

Frustrated, Steve got out of his boat and walked over to him.

"I told you, I don't want--"

"Huh?" The trader said, offering a chest.

Steve looked at the contents.

There were some green things, called fungi, some red leaves, called crimson forest leaves, and some torches that looked they had soul sand blocks where there was usually wood. But most of the chest's contents were not anything he'd seen before.

"What is this?" He asked the trader.

"Huh," the trader said, looking towards the Nether portal that glowed purple, the doorway clear amidst its obsidian blocks.

"The Nether?" Steve asked.

"Huh."

Steve turned back to the trader.

"Okay," he said. "I'll take the fungi and the soul torches for fifty diamonds."

"Huh."

The items were transferred to Steve's inventory and the fifty diamonds went to the trader.

Then the trader began rowing back out to sea.

Looking at his stuff, Steve remained unable to understand the things he'd just traded fifty diamonds for.

A mine cart rattled past him just then, powered by its redstone circuits, carrying lumps of coal. Another followed carrying gold, from one of the other tunnels that were lit night and day with torches.

He walked back to his house.

The greenery outside was peaceful and refreshing. He always liked his farms.

Stepping through the front door, he saw a fire was crackling. Torches lit up the room. The ceiling here was hollow, for above were his books and potions. A wooden stairway connected the levels.

Glass windows allowed him to see his farms and the XP farm he'd built some time ago.

Then Sean, his dog, bounded over.

He had found him not long after he had established this colony. Sean had been standing amidst a field of trees and stalks that was now his home.

Steve petted him and held out a piece of meat.

Sean ate it happily, and sat down, wagging his tail.

Smiling, Steve walked up the stairs to the alchemists' room and to his rows of chests.

He opened one.

It contained gold and diamond weapons, tools, gold and diamonds themselves, bread, potions, end eyes, redstone, and other things he'd mined.

He placed the stuff he'd gotten from the trader in and closed the chest.

He walked over to the crafting table.

There were recipes for the fungi and the torches he'd traded diamonds for.

The fungi required a specific nylium, which he didn't have.

He wanted to craft more soul torches.

The ones he had glowed brightly, and it almost hurt his eyes to look at them.

He placed the soul sand blocks and the oak on the table, and they merged to form a soul torch.

Too bright, he added it to his inventory, and then crafted a hundred.

Then he left his house again.

He walked past the carrot farm, then the potato farm. The XP farm was working well. Enders and spiders were spawning at the top of a nearby dark tower and being sent down. He slew two spiders, and collected the points.

Steve's three mining tunnels were churning out carts of gold, diamond, and coal every few moments.

As he walked past the stables and the villagers' huts, something standing beside the gold mine caught his eye.

He turned and looked to see a person standing there. The person's shirt was green, his pants blue. He had black hair, black eyes, and a still face, with no smile, no smirk, no frown.

He seemed to be staring straight at Steve, when he suddenly turned and darted for the Nether portal.

"Hey! Who are you?" Steve shouted at the figure, but the figure did not respond.

Then it hit him.

He remembered tales the villagers had told him, about this silent person who sometimes appeared around them, never saying anything, never looking angry or happy. Every time he was there, he would build something before leaving. He made pyramids, houses, ships, and castles. Some of the villagers had been too afraid to check the ships and castles, so they burned them. They did manage to use the houses, and the pyramids were just edifices of stone and sand.

They called the stranger Herobrine.

Herobrine jumped through the portal before Steve could say another word.

Steve was about to run after him when he remembered. The

Nether had changed. One day, he had gone ghast hunting, when he realized the realm had entirely changed. There were still the wastelands, flowing with lava and crawling with mobs, but something about it was different. The mobs were darker, the Nether Fortresses more numerous, and the terrain had changed. Afraid, Steve had run back and nearly closed the portal. Since then, he had not left the Overworld.

But the trader had gone there, most likely, and he was fine. And he had soul torches and fungi, supposedly from the Nether, where he had not found either before.

He checked his inventory. He had his diamond pickaxe, shield, and a bunch of torches with him.

He ran for his house.

Sean was there, barking.

"Hey, Sean, I'm going to the Nether," he said as he armed himself with his diamond sword, adding another to his own inventory. Then he equipped some fifty pieces of bread, and fifty torches.

He turned away from his chests.

Sean looked at him, happy, but then sensed he was leaving and whined.

"Sorry, Sean, but I gotta go. There's something I need to find out." He ran out from his house and to the Nether portal.

Standing before the great obsidian blocks and the rippling purple Golden Gate, Steve braced himself.

Drawing his sword, he closed his eyes, and ran through.

Chapter 2: The Adventure Begins

Steve heard the crunch of the soles of his diamond boots as he landed on red blocks of the Nether.

The purple portal rippled and moved behind him, amidst the red and molten wastelands.

A hill cascaded down from where he was, just as it always did. Some skeletons were crawling around, armed with their bows. A lava waterfall flowed from a red cliff, towards a pool of lava that glowed bright and orange.

He spotted a hill of obsidian blocks to his right but there was no more sign of Herobrine.

Then he remembered the piglins and switched his helmet to a golden one. At least, now, he wouldn't be attacked by them.

He started down the hill, away from the portal. Herobrine couldn't have gone far, but he did seem to teleport here and there. His blank, unmoving face had always chilled Steve to the bone, but he was determined to find him now.

But Herobrine, and the new Nether, it was just too confusing. Steve didn't like things to be confusing. He found that he felt safe whenever he could control a situation. With the old Nether, he knew what mobs there were, how to fight them, run from them, or not be detected by them. In the Overworld, he trusted that torches would keep the mobs away, and that he was safe as long as he had light. These new things were just troubling.

He reached the bottom of the hill before long, and stood by a pool of lava that probably drained beneath the ground.

To the right was a range of crimson trees and obsidian mountains. To the far left was more lava. Steve decided he'd walk the cooler path for now.

Walking carefully around the pool of lava, he reached one of the obsidian hills and began climbing.

He heard the far-off shriek of a ghast, then the hiss of a spider. But these sounds didn't concern him. He was used to these.

When he reached the top of the hill, he turned and saw his portal standing where it had always been, and looked back to see a field of skeletons.

"Seriously?" He whispered to himself.

There were piglins too, armed with crossbows, but that didn't mean anything. He had his golden helmet. But the skeletons would still attack him.

Then an arrow raced past him and struck one of the obsidian blocks.

"Ah!" He shouted, jumping aside.

More arrows began raining down around him.

Shouting, Steve jumped from the hill.

As he fell through the air, the skeletons began turning their bows up to follow him.

He glimpsed a red flash and felt a stab of pain as one of the arrows hit him.

Shouting, he landed with a thud.

Another red flash.

He quickly equipped his shield as the skeletons continued to loose their arrows at him.

As he raised his green, white, and orange painted shield, the arrows struck it instead of him.

"Hah!" He shouted, running at one. He struck the skeleton

with his diamond sword. A few hits and the skeleton went up as a puff of smoke.

He turned toward another. Forgetting, he lowered his shield for a moment and an arrow struck his golden helmet.

"Ah!" He shouted, raising his shield again.

If his helmet was hit too many times, he would lose it, and then the piglins would be attacking him as well.

He put away his sword. Arrows fell harmlessly around him, while one or two struck his shield.

He started planting the soul torches he'd gotten from the trader. A line of blue flame was glowing within seconds.

Now, he thought, even if I lose my helmet, the piglins won't attack me.

But he didn't have to wait to lose his helmet. With the soul torches burning, they were already drawing away.

He drew his sword again and started fighting the rest of skeletons. Before long, all of them were gone, and Steve still had his golden helmet.

But he was mildly wounded, so he ate some of his bread. He felt better, then ran over to the other range of obsidian hills.

He looked at the red ground. There was no sign of the battle he'd just fought. There were only the soul torches.

This'll be my base, he decided. I shall call it, the Vale of Bones.

He opened his inventory and crafted a crafting table with oak blocks.

He retrieved it from his inventory and walked to the line of soul torches.

He dropped the table nearby.

Then, with it, he crafted a sign.

He walked back to the hill, ascended to its height, and placed the sign there. He wrote The Vale of Bones.

Smiling, he headed back to the crafting table.

"I think I'm gonna be here awhile," Steve said, happy with the battle. It reminded him that he could face anything. "Time to build a shelter."

Chapter 3: Crafting

I need supplies, Steve decided, and I think I'll bring Sean. This place seems safe enough for him, and I won't let him out.

Turning, with his shield already equipped, he drew his golden sword and ran.

Steve hurried to the hill just a few blocks away, ran up, and then down again.

He could see his portal.

He was there in a few moments and ran through.

He landed back on the green grass and felt the warm rays of the sun on his face. Steve felt refreshed. The trees, the animals, and the birds were a happy sight. It always was for someone returning from the Nether.

He ran to his house.

The villagers were busy with their own things, the pigs were eating, and the horses were looking out from their stalls.

Carts of gold and iron ingots rattled and the XP farm was trapping ever more mobs as he reached the front door.

Inside, he found Sean barking happily to see him, his tail wagging.

Steve pet him.

"Ready for an adventure?" He asked Sean. "We're going to the Nether. We're gonna find Herobrine and solve this mystery once and for all."

He walked up to his room of books and chests.

Then he picked up fifty stacks of meat, some more wood, cobblestone, and iron.

He headed back to the front door, with Sean following.

Steve picked up the leash and started back for the portal.

Seconds later, they were amidst the red wastelands.

With oak and cobblestone blocks, Steve built a little home for himself.

He used the iron ingots to make a door, and the oak to build a staircase, with a landing halfway up from the ground. He placed torches beside every corner of the first level, then he crafted a chest, and placed it on the landing, by the stairs.

The fire torches of the first level were a comforting light, unlike the harsh orange of the lava fountains and rivers.

Next, he went upstairs, carrying torches, and placed one above the chest.

He placed another at the opposite end, flanking the single glass pane he was using as a window, and one more behind the stairs.

Sean was watching him happily as the house materialized around him.

Before long, Steve was standing by Sean, the torches crackling away to keep mobs from spawning, the soul torches shining outside to keep piglins away, and the oak and cobblestone walls keeping them safe.

Steve tossed Sean a piece of meat, and the dog ate it hungrily.

Then he headed to his crafting table and crafted a furnace.

He placed it beside the crafting table. He added chicken and wood, and the meat began to cook.

It was done soon, and he ate it at once.

Sean was beside him.

"Okay, you stay here, Sean," Steve told him. "I've still got to search for this Herobrine."

Steve walked towards the door.

Sean did not follow.

The line of soul torches was still burning blue at the side of the house.

From the outside, it was not a comforting sight, being a partly wooden sanctuary amidst a burning inferno and all that.

Steve turned toward where he'd placed the sign marking this area.

He saw Herobrine standing there, face still as it always was.

The sight sent a chill running down Steve's spine.

Then a great pyramid appeared before him.

Steve jumped back, startled.

The pyramid was a staggering height of stone. There was a door, and the tunnel was lit with torches.

Steve turned back to look for Herobrine, but he was gone.

Steve jumped up and ran for the hill. Racing up the obsidian blocks, he reached the signpost, but Herobrine was nowhere to be seen.

Chapter 4: Warning

Steve eyed the pyramid, sword drawn. There was nothing truly ominous about the thing, except for the fact that some ghostly creature had just dropped it without even building it.

It looked normal, though it did not feel that way.

Steve approached it, weary.

The doorway was still there and still lit by a line of torches.

Where they led, Steve could not say.

He was soon standing directly before it.

Despite the torchlight, fear froze him.

"He's never really done anything bad," he said to himself. "All he does is build things and look from afar. He probably isn't really bad. I'm just being silly."

He made himself walk forward past the first two torches, then the second set. He walked straight ahead, looking back to see if the way would close or something was happening.

Before long, he was at a stone stairwell, illuminated by torches.

He looked back through the doorway one more time..

Then he turned and started up the stairs.

He couldn't see what was at the top, but there was nowhere here for anything to spawn or hide.

With more confidence, he reached the top to find a glowing and rippling purple panel surrounded by obsidian blocks. Torches

17

illuminated the area as well.

Steve stared at the portal. This would lead to only one place: the Overworld. Why was Herobrine wanting him to go there? Steve had already traveled much of the Overworld and seen the desert wastelands and the frozen north. Like everyone else, he knew the rest of the world like the back of his hand.

Part of him wanted to run, to leave this pyramid, get TNT, and demolish it, but a part of him wanted to go through the portal.

He looked down at the bottom of the steps.

He could see the torches at each landing glowing brightly.

Sean's safe there, he told himself. He'll be fine. I'll be back soon, anyway.

He turned back to the portal. Glowing purple, it continued to shine and shimmer, white tendrils of smoke floating amidst the Golden Gate.

Steve braced himself and walked through.

He emerged amidst a desolate wasteland. The sun shone brightly. There were no trees, no animals, and no greenery of any kind. There was only the desert and its staggering sand dunes.

The sunlight glinted off Steve's diamond and gold armor, and he squinted to see a cave, towards the north.

There were no torches there, only darkness amidst a sea of light.

He saw a creeper, just one, roaming aimlessly.

Suddenly Herobrine appeared, right before Steve.

Steve jumped back, startled.

He raised his sword.

"Who are you?" He shouted.

Herobrine did not move or speak.

"What are you?" Steve shouted at him.

He could feel his fear rising.

"Speak!" Steve shouted, fighting the feeling to run, get back to the Nether, demolish the pyramid, and try to forget all about Herobrine.

Herobrine lifted a hand, and pointed towards the cave.

Steve looked at the yawning darkness.

"No," he shook his head, "I'm not going there."

Herobrine had disappeared and was not there to hear him.

"There's no way I'm going there," Steve said.

He turned towards the portal, when he heard the muttering of a villager.

He turned to see a group of them walking past the cave, herding llamas, sheep, and camels.

Steve watched.

They were walking past him, so he looked to the east. There was nothing but sand and sand.

"Hey!" He shouted at them. "What is this place?"

The villagers looked at him. Some of them muttered that strange language he'd been able to learn.

But all he could hear was, "Secret."

The crowd moved on, leaving Steve.

Steve looked at the cave.

"What secret?"

Villagers weren't dangerous, and if they were, he could fight, Steve told himself.

He decided he would see the cave.

Equipped with his sword and shield, he started towards the darkness. The creeper that seemed to be guarding the place saw him, and began walking towards him.

Steve struck it twice with his sword and the creeper went up as a cloud of smoke.

Then there was just the cave.

Steve put away his sword and equipped a torch.

The light illuminated the ground up to a few blocks ahead.

Beyond it was darkness.

Steve stepped forward.

He placed the torch on the ground, then placed another by the right wall, and then another by the left one. Walking forward, he placed torches as he went. The cave was built of stone blocks. There were spider webs some dozen blocks away, but no spider.

Steve placed a few more torches and walked on. He equipped his sword again.

Then he heard the hiss of a spider and it appeared before him, red eyes bright.

It lunged, but Steve jumped aside and slashed.

The spider hissed at him.

It attacked, and Steve stabbed it.

The spider blinked red and shrieked, as Steve struck again and the thing went up in smoke.

Turning back to the rest of the cave, he placed another torch where he was, and continued walking.

He went past the spider webs.

Then Herobrine appeared.

Steve was ready to strike him.

"What is this?" He asked.

"A war is brewing," Herobrine responded. "The One is marshaling his forces. There will be no stopping him."

"What are you talking about?"

"The universe is a cosmic sea, where all things are hidden. The One is the true god, not the others. The others are false."

Steve looked at him with rage.

He was about to strike him when Herobrine said, "An Ender dragon has been released. For the first time it roams beyond its own portal. And now it flies about the Nether. Watch out for your friend."

Steve's eyes widened.

Almost paralyzed with fear, Steve forced himself to turn around and head for the portal.

He could see the outside, but the cave was dissolving around him. He ran, running past the torches as they fell away into darkness.

He emerged from the cave as it disappeared and left nothing but the sandy plains.

Steve almost fell as he ran toward the obsidian Golden Gate.

He thundered though with his sword and shield.

Emerging from the Golden Gate, his eyes widened at the sight of an Ender dragon circling above his house. Its purple eyes were staring at the building as its wings flapped.

The pyramid was still there, and he could hear Sean barking.

Steve looked at the house. The only window was upstairs, and Sean wasn't there.

He might've been with the chests, but Steve couldn't tell.

"Hey, you!" Steve shouted, and the dragon spun to see him, eyes glaring.

"Yeah, you!" Steve yelled, when the dragon spotted him.

"Leave my friend alone!"

The dragon roared and rushed toward him.

It swooped low, flying just over his head.

Steve ducked.

He retrieved one of his potions, a potion of strength. He drank it, and cast the beaker aside.

He felt the potion coursing through his system.

With all his strength and lives, he turned to see the dragon rushing toward him from the hill where his portal was.

"How did this get here?" He asked himself. The Ender dragon was not a creature of the Nether or the Overworld. It was of another realm, and it couldn't cross to the former. And yet…

The dragon rushed towards him again.

This time, Steve struck its wing as it flew past, shrieking. The beast blinked red, but Steve knew it would take more than a few hits to slay the dragon.

Sean was still barking. He was at the window now, watching Steve battle the dragon.

For hours, Steve and the dragon fought. Once, Steve was hit and fell to the ground, but he got back up, with only half a life lost. The potion had already worn out, and Steve still fought with his enchanted diamond sword. He had his infinibow with him as well, but an enchanted sword would deal out more damage than a bow, even an enchanted one.

The dragon was still flying, seemingly unaffected by the fight. But Steve knew he was. It would only be a matter of time now.

Before long, Steve struck its wing again and the dragon collapsed. Lying on the ground, it shrieked one more ominous shriek, and then its head fell to the ground.

Steve eyed the beast, its purple eyes no longer glowing.

He had lost all but one life.

Steve ate some of the cooked meat he had with him, and at once regained all of his lives.

He walked toward his house, Sean still barking.

He opened the door and found Sean at the door.

"Hey, Sean!" He said, petting him. "I'm sorry I left you here. I never should have followed that thing."

Steve thought over the cave, what Herobrine had told him, and this. None of it made sense.

He didn't like the pyramid either.

He got some blocks of dynamite, and walked out again to the pyramid.

He placed two blocks at each side of the pyramid, and a few higher up.

Then he lit one of them and ran back.

The blocks of TNT went off with loud roars that echoed off

the obsidian blocks.

Chunks of the pyramid disappeared with clouds of smoke, and soon, there was nothing left.

Steve looked at where the pyramid had been. A few blocks from the ground had gone with it, when the TNT blocks touching them had gone off.

He noticed that portal was still there.

Steve equipped his pickaxe and went to it. He built a stone stairway up, mined one of the obsidian blocks, and the Golden Gate disappeared. It was nothing now.

Then he headed back to his house.

"We'll rest for a while," he told Sean, "then I'm going out again. But I'm gonna have to send you back home."

Sean had been happy as always, but he whined when he heard that.

"Don't worry," he told his friend, "I'll only be here for a few more days."

Sean ate some meat, while Steve ate some cooked pork and bread.

He stayed with Sean upstairs.

An hour went by, and he looked up from his book to see out the window. The site where the pyramid had been was fissured, and he could see the portal, with one obsidian block missing.

Steve continued to read.

Chapter 5: Mobs and Tree

Hours had gone by, but the sky had not changed. It would be morning now, Steve knew, but here, there was no night or day. There weren't the comforting rays of the sun or the sight of greenery and farms, but the red, molten wastelands.

His shield was equipped and Sean was sitting by him. It almost looked like he was smiling.

"Mornin', Sean," Steve said.

He got up and petted him.

"Alright, time for you to get back home to the Overworld," he said.

He picked up Sean's leash and walked downstairs, where the crafting table, furnace, and chest were, and they walked outside. There were no mobs to be seen.

For that, Steve was grateful.

They walked towards the hill where the portal was and climbed up.

They walked through the portal.

It was raining.

The torches burned bright, but the sky was dark and gloomy. Torches burned at all the windows of his stone and oaken house.

The horses whinnied, but the streets were deserted, with everyone seeking shelter from the rain.

The farm was growing nicely, and the XP farm was still

trapping mobs.

Steve walked over to collect them.

Then he headed straight for his house.

He and Sean stepped through the front door and Steve let go of the leash.

He walked to his room of books and chests.

He equipped himself with some more food, oak panels, stone, a few more enchanted weapons, and some golden armor.

He walked back to the door.

"Alright, you stay here. Guard the house. I'll be back soon," he told Sean.

He fed him one more piece of meat, then turned to leave.

He walked straight for the portal.

He was back at his other house within moments.

"Alright," he muttered to himself, "there's a world here to explore, and questions that need to be answered. I can always head back home to resupply, so that isn't a problem."

With shield and enchanted sword, he set out towards the other hill range. He climbed up to where he'd placed the sign, and walked past.

A river of lava was flowing past the obsidian banks.

To the right, he spotted a cliff where the lava poured from.

He walked down the hill and to the bank of the river.

He placed one block of stone at the bank, then another in front of that. He placed more as he walked, and was soon across.

He kept walking, past more obsidian, past skeletons roaming blocks away that did not see him. Soon, he saw a piglin, but he was wearing golden armor so he wasn't attacked.

He checked what stuff his line of inventory had.

There were torches, oak, and stone, as far as he was willing to trade.

He walked up to the piglin.

It was carrying a crossbow.

He saw what the piglin had.

Steve traded twenty planks of oak for fifty warped fungi, nylium, and bone meal.

He knew the materials had to be mixed to be anything, so he placed the nylium on the ground, mixed the bone meal with the fungi, and added it to the nylium.

Nothing happened.

He got up and left the thing. Perhaps it would change by the morrow.

He continued walking.

An hour later, he found a crimson grove. Crimson leaves ornamented the great trees and branches. The same fungi the trader had traded with him the day before was nearby, green amidst the crimson.

So, it'll grow, he thought to himself.

He spent hours roaming the new Nether. With his golden armor, no piglins attacked him, and he easily slew any skeleton that crossed his path.

To mark the trail back to his house, he left soul torches every twenty blocks.

Now, he placed another beside a lake of lava. There was a lavafall some way to the far right.

As he walked past, he heard the shriek of a ghast and turned, sword drawn. The ghast was gliding toward him, red eyes glowing.

"Alright, let's fight," Steve said, a veteran of a thousand ghast fights. With the hundreds of times he'd been here, he'd fought hundreds more of these things. Strangely, the ghast was comforting amidst this unfamiliar land, since it was something that he was used to. The ghast shrieked again.

It launched a round of fire at him. But Steve didn't jump aside. He let the fire race toward him, crackling as it sped through the air.

Then he struck it with his blade and the round of fire went soaring back through the air, hitting the ghast. The mob shrieked, blinking red, then fired another round.

Steve deflected this one as well, and the ghast turned and fell to the ground, then went up in a cloud of smoke.

"Easy," Steve said, turning back to the bunch of crimson trees he had been walking toward.

He walked on past them.

He continued walking till he noticed a wall of obsidian. It loomed twenty blocks above the red ground, shrouded by a red and orange glow.

Then he noticed the towers that rose higher still from the wall. They weren't the clean, square towers of the stone castles of the Overworld. These towers were staggered, gnarled, and unfriendly.

There was a single archway to let people, or mobs, through.

It looked like there were fire torches burning. That was a comfort. The soul torches chased away piglins and felt like a better defense against the worse mobs, even though they weren't. Fire torches felt like home, felt like safety. That allowed for more strength than sorcery.

He walked to the arch.

There was the same red ground.

From there, he could see over the wall, the lavafall, crimson trees, and the red air.

Then he spied a crafting table. There was also a furnace, and shelves, an array of potions, and some other stuff.

"Someone lives here," Steve muttered, when he spotted Herobrine standing across the ground, next to one of the shelves.

Steve felt fear stab through him. He wanted to run just then, but something stopped him.

"Who are you?" He said.

Herobrine didn't respond.

He just stepped to the side.

Then Steve saw it.

The dispensers along the walls.

"Really?" Steve said, as arrows began to fly out from the dispensers.

Steve turned and ran, the arrows racing past harmlessly and then striking the obsidian wall.

He was beyond the castle within moments and ran still further.

Before long, he found his trail of soul torches and followed them back to his house.

"So he lives here?" Steve asked himself as he ran.

It didn't make any sense.

There was just some random freak living here who went up to the surface to stand around and materialize things out of thin air?

Who would live here?

Who could build like that?

Was it one of those potions?"

Steve still couldn't figure it out by the time he got back to his house.

The soul torches and fire torches were still burning.

He stepped through the door and went upstairs.

He looked out the window. Herobrine's home was not that far away, only about a thousand blocks. Somehow, this world didn't feel as safe as it did. Well, that had already been the case when the Ender dragon showed up. But now it was worse.

Steve turned away from the window, hoping he wouldn't see Herobrine for some time.

Chapter 6: Railroad

Steve didn't go out again for a few hours. He ate some chicken and bread and then went over his stuff. He already had twenty-two stacks of oak, nine blocks of stone, ten more pieces each of chicken, mutton, and bread, twenty soul torches, thirty fire torches, and his weapons with him.

His one chest contained more oak and stone, more food, and some healing potions.

He wouldn't have to resupply for some time.

There was no night again, no time to sleep, no cool clean air and greenery, or the moon of night. There was only that red glare, the lava, the obsidian, and a red sky.

Steve found he had never disliked the Nether more, not even when he first saw it.

All he knew about the Nether when he was living at Golden Gate were the things his friends and fellow townsfolk told him. He had heard tales of the mobs, the lava rivers, the heaps and hills of obsidian. His parents didn't allow him to go there, because he was too young to meet the dangers of that world. However, before he'd left as a colonizer to establish this town, he went on his first trip to the Nether. He did not like it. Where there were usually trees, there were streams of lava. Where there were birds, there were ghasts. Where there were people, there were piglins. Where there was blue sky, there was a red glare.

But, Steve, had to admit, there were some things that were brilliant about the Nether. There was obsidian all around, and there were many chances to combat great mobs and prove yourself a hero.

The resources found there were crucial to many of the builders' works, whose supplies were transported from here to there by more than fifty portals. All of the portals led to mines and mining towns that had been built by the people of Golden Gate, the city at the center of the world, and all of them were guarded by warriors.

Steve still hadn't been able to find any of Golden Gate's portals or mines.

He remembered the railway that the king was building. Only a third of it had been built. It spanned rivers of lava, rose above the obsidian hills, and then ran at ground level. The railway started at North Mine. Master cartographers had been able to map the Nether, and correspond it to their world. Each mine was really ten thousand blocks away from Golden Gate.

The railway had already branched and was joining up with the lines from the mines North-North-West and North-North-East. Carts were already stored, ready for deployment when the rail was complete. The council had degreed that having portals for everything was not practical. One could not determine where the portal would lead to, and the mines needed to be at specific locations, so some of the mines were more remote than the others. These rails, powered by redstone, would allow the mines with no portal to send carts to the nearest mines with portals, to be teleported back to Golden Gate.

Steve wondered how the people who spent their days mining away at rock, obsidian, and stone managed to defend themselves from the terrors of this world.

They have guards, silly, he told himself, guards armed with infinibows and enchanted swords, and gold armor.

I have some golden armor, an infinibow, a sword, and some

food, roaming along the new Nether, with almost no idea of what I'm doing.

He shook his head and retrieved the map of the new Nether that Cartographer Wilkins had given him before he left. His house was twenty thousand blocks west of Golden Gate.

The far west mine was a quarry, marked with the pictures of a block of dynamite and a pickaxe.

The map showed the railway going north, then turning west, then north again, across a lava river, than going straight for five thousand blocks, then turning west and running to North-North-West Mine, where it was marked with more dynamite and a pickax.

The western mine itself was twenty thousand blocks from Steve's base. He could get there before too long.

He put away the map away and checked his weapons. Their health was still good, and they wouldn't break for some time. The enchanted sword was comparatively undamaged, even though he'd used it to fight the Ender dragon..

He left his home and started west.

The obsidian ranges were monotonous and boring, and soon he wasn't even noticing them anymore. A few piglins wandered amongst the blocks, but none of them paid him any mind.

A ghast shrieked about five hundred blocks away. It didn't see him, and Steve was not looking for a fight. He just kept walking.

Every now and then, he would look around to see if Herobrine was there. After the case with the dispensers, Steve was sure Herobrine didn't mean anything good. And yet, he had warned Steve when the Ender dragon attacked Steve's house where his friend was.

The tale of Herobrine was well-known at Golden Gate. The townsfolk always spoke of him, though the council and the king disregarded it as just tales. For a long time, Steve had not believed it either. And yet here Steve was, contemplating what Herobrine could be, and making sure he wasn't near.

It was a few hours and a few pieces of bread later when Steve caught sight of the mine.

It was a fair sight, better than any he'd seen for a long time.

Guards with golden armor and enchanted weapons stood sentry at the gates and the railway.

A few miners were mulling about. The rest were working.

Steve reached the gate a few moments later.

"Who are you?" One of the guards asked.

"I'm Steve, from Golden Gate."

"Right, you're Colonizer James' son, aren't you?"

"Yup."

"Well, you're welcome any time," the guard said, smiling, "but I don't see why you'd wanna be here. It isn't exactly a tourist spot."

"Well, I decided I'd look around the new Nether. Have you happened to see an Ender dragon or Herobrine?"

The guard's face turned serious.

"Actually, we did. The dragon flew by yesterday. We didn't dare attack it. I'm sorry, if we'd known there was someone here, we would've fought."

"I know. Don't worry."

"We also saw Herobrine."

It was Steve's turn to turn serious.

"He popped up here, not far from where you're standing, all silent and blank as always. Then he left that."

The guard pointed to a pyramid of TNT.

"Yeah, I know," the guard said, when he saw Steve's look. "We were afraid it was going to go off so we cleared the mine and started running. Only, it never did. The Chief Miner wants to use it for the mine, but the captain says no one's to go near it."

"Well, I agree," Steve said. "You're sure this is safe?"

"Safe enough. Captain said that if one of us thought something was going to go wrong, sound the alarm, and we'll evacuate with the mine-carts."

Steve nodded.

He left the guards and walked through the gate.

Another guard was standing by the door to a building.

"Breakroom", the sign read.

Steve went to it.

He nodded at the guards and walked up the oak planks.

Light was shining through the windows and he could see about a dozen miners eating and talking.

He opened the door and walked in.

The herald on his sleeve told the miners he was from Golden Gate.

"Hey, I'm Henry. Nice to meet you," one of the miners said as he stood up. "What's a colonizer doing here?"

"I'm looking around the new Nether. Things have changed."

"Sure have," another miner said from one of the benches. It was an old man with white hair and squinting eyes, a tankard of milk by his side. "Just two days ago we saw a great beast. Breathed fire and burnt the land, he did."

"Oh, don't go speaking nonsense again," another miner said. "We just saw an Ender dragon. But how did it get here? Didn't happen to see it, did you?"

"I did."

"You slew it?"

"Yes."

"Well, then you're a hero. An Ender Dragon is difficult to fight."

"And not many Enders show up here," Steve said.

"Sir," he said to the barkeep, "I'd like some milk."

"Right away," the man nodded.

The barkeep turned, picked up a tankard, and held it to one of the barrels' taps. Ice-chilled milk flowed from the tap.

"Here you go," he said, setting the cup on the bar.

"Thanks."

Steve picked it up and drank.

It was cold and refreshing, and after that long walk through lakes of lava, across wastelands, and past heaps of obsidian, the breakroom and fellow people of Golden Gate were a welcome sight.

"Where you headed?" Henry asked as Steve drank.

He set the cup on the bar again.

"I thought I might travel with the obsidian and stones for a while. I understand the line between here and North Mine is operational?"

"Sure is. You can go with the driver, though it won't be too comfortable."

"Well, none of the Nether is comfortable."

The miners laughed.

"What about these fungi and crimson trees?" Steve asked when they'd quieted again.

"Yeah, we don't know much about those," Henry said. "You'd probably know more from one of the libraries."

Steve nodded.

"Thanks," he said.

He turned to the barkeep.

"Here's some bread. Thanks for the milk."

The barkeep nodded.

"Thanks for what you told me. I'll be leaving soon," he told the miners.

"Report to a driver's cart," Henry said. "Just go past here, to the mine, and wait till you see a train ready to depart. The first cart's the one you're looking for."

Steve nodded, and walked out the door.

He nodded at the guards again and turned to go, the soles of his shoes crunching the sand and dust of the cobble road.

He could see the railway from here.

It was a grand feat of engineering. The first mile, it seemed, went from the pinnacle of a hill to another, then rose up to avoid a higher mountain, and then Steve couldn't see any more.

As he approached the mine, he heard the miners talking as they chipped away with their tools. He could hear carts rattling from the furthest sections of the mine.

Steve looked to see someone sitting in the first cart of a line of twenty, some few yards back, all carrying obsidian. The man, the driver, as Henry had called him, was armored with golden plate and helmet, and was armed with a shield
and enchanted sword.

He pushed a lever and the first cart moved forward, its wheels squeaking just slightly as it lurched. The chain between that one and the second grew taut, and the second cart began to move. Soon, the entire line was barreling out of the station, which was a structure of stone. The building had a few windows, and through them Steve could see people scratching at papers and a man speaking to the committee.

He walked up to the station.

Walking over the line, he approached the stationmaster.

"When will the next line of carts be leaving?" He asked.

"About five minutes," the armed and gold-plated fellow responded. "Why? You don't look like a miner or a driver."

"Well I'm not. I'm a colonizer, but Henry said I could travel with a driver to North-North-West Mine."

"He did, did he?"

"Yeah."

"Well, then, go ahead. Henry's Chief of Transportation around here."

Steve nodded.

The mine actually made the Nether seemed pleasant, like an oasis amidst the scorched plains of the desert. There was drink and food, even ice. Most important of all, there were familiar people. The two days that Steve had spent here had been disquieting. Herobrine, the dragon, and just the air of the Nether itself, was almost too much. Other people, and other voices, they helped Steve's nerves.

The line of carts arrived five minutes later, as the stationmaster said it would, with a second one following.

"Driver Thorn, this colonizer here says Chief Henry allows him a seat with a driver," he said.

Thorn looked at him. His eyes squinted and his face looked like stone.

"Well, the track is quiet. There aren't many mobs to fight, and I'm grateful, but I can get bored. You'll be welcome," he said, smiling.

Thorn's name was quite deceptive. So was his appearance. He looked like the sort who would always be complaining and muttering. His actions seemed quite the opposite, though. He was friendly. He was also old, but when he smiled, he did not look tired.

"Thank you," Steve said to the stationmaster, before walking to the cart.

The lead cart was comfortable, with a bench and a barrel of chilled milk and a tankard anchored to it.

Steve opened the iron door and stepped aboard.

He shut the panel, then latched it.

"Ready?" Thorn asked him.

Steve nodded.

Thorn pushed the lever, his shield before him.

"Leaving station," he said, and the cart lurched forward.

Steve could feel the engine running as the wheels squeaked. The chain that connected the manager's cart to the first carrier cart clinked as it grew taut.

The second cart moved forward, then the third, and then the fourth and fifth. A speedometer showed that the train was moving at five miles per hour.

Soon the needle arced toward ten, then thirteen, then fifteen, and then the cart was barreling along at thirty.

The station grew further away as the carts sped off the sheer cliff, racing for the next one.

Steve looked behind and saw the second train following.

He looked down and saw the railway as a blur. The vale of obsidian was the same as any other, but it was far below.

"Don't look down, friend," Thorn said, when he saw Steve's face. "Makes you dizzy."

The train reached the pinnacle of the other mountain, and was clear of it before Steve could blink.

"So, how long have you been a driver?"

"Since this mine opened. About three years," the man said.

"So, since before the Nether changed?"

"Yeah."

"Have you noticed anything odd about the Nether?"

"Odd?" The driver raised his brow. "A little. Saw an Ender dragon once."

"Like the one two days ago?" Steve asked.

"Yup."

They roared past a hill of obsidian and a bunch of crimson trees.

"Have you seen Herobrine?" Steve asked a moment later.

"Aye," Thorn replied. "He showed up at the mine two days ago and left that pile of dynamite. About three weeks ago, after we'd gone back to Golden Gate, I was walking home when I saw him. He was standing at the highest level of the Great Tower. All still and silent. Then he left."

The Great Tower was Golden Gate's watchtower. Anyone was allowed to look from there, and from there they could see the streets, castles, libraries, sentry posts, and the harbor with its ships and the running track. They could also see beyond the city, to the green plains and hills. At night, torches burned outside the city, though the light from Golden Gate itself was enough to keep mobs from spawning nearby.

Steve thought about what Thorn had told him. Things were seriously getting worse, and Herobrine was not a friend.

"Herobrine is a danger to us," Steve said. "Yesterday, I was walking around the Nether, heading north from New Beacon's portal, and found this obsidian castle. Though, it was just towers and the parapets. But beyond that I found a crafting table, a furnace, books, and potions. And there were dispensers along the walls. Herobrine appeared. I tried to talk to him but then the arrows started flying so I ran. I haven't seen Herobrine since, and I don't want to."

"Can't disagree with you there," Thorn said. "Folk like that ain't nothing but trouble. He's always been a bother, anyway, showing up out of nowhere, and leaving stuff behind. Most of the time, that stuff is helpful, though."

"He left this pyramid near my house that I built near the portal. There was a portal at the highest floor. I went through and was transported to a desert. There was this cave, and then a crowd walking by. I went to the cave, where a creeper was walking around. I slew a spider and kept walking. I couldn't find anything, but then Herobrine said something about a war, about the One. Then he warned me an Ender dragon was attacking my house, where I'd left my dog. So I ran back and slew the dragon. Herobrine was warning me. That doesn't make sense."

"Well—" Thorn said, but quickly spun around when he heard shrieks of ghasts.

The mobs glided through the air, their red eyes looking at

Thorn and Steve.

Steve and Thorn rose, the former with an enchanted blade, the latter with a bow.

"We cannot let these ghasts hit the cart," Thorn said, as another appeared. "If they do, we'll be flung off with it. And it's a sheer drop from here."

It was true. The carts were running about three hundred blocks above floor of obsidian.

If they fell, they would either be badly injured or die. It would be troublesome to get back onto the tracks.

"Okay," Steve said, "you hit the left one with your bow. I'll handle the right one."

Thorn nodded, and began loosing arrows at the left ghast. The mob began blinking red as the arrows hit.

Steve focused on the other one as the ghasts shrieked again, chasing the carts.

"We're almost at the lava river," Thorn warned.

The right ghast launched a round of fire at the cart.

Thorn loosed an arrow at the left one as Steve watched the fire race toward the cart.

Then he struck it with his sword and the fire raced back toward the ghast. It hit the mob. The ghast fell away and Thorn loosed another arrow at the last one.

Then the ghast launched a round of fire, but before Steve could strike it, the fire hit the third cart.

A cacophony of noises erupted as the links broke and several of the carts flew off the rail. Stones, obsidian, and ingots rained from the falling carts as Steve and Thorn held on to theirs.

Two of the carts were still linked to the driver's. All three of them had risen up when the rest were thrown off. Now they crashed back on the rails.

Steve fell forward as the cart stabilized.

A moment went by, then Thorn was shouting at him.

"Get up, Steve!"

Steve stood up, and saw that the ghast was still chasing them.

"This fight isn't over," Thorn said.

Steve turned to the mob.

Thorn launched a bunch of arrows at the ghast, when it launched another orb of fire.

Trailing smoke and flame, the projectile raced toward the three carts.

Steve struck it with his sword.

The fire raced back, hit the ghast, and sent the mob falling to the ground.

Steve turned to Thorn.

"Haven't seen mobs for some time, huh?" He asked him.

Thorn's face was grim.

"This is the first since three months ago, when my cart was attacked by three ghasts. But that was near North Mine, and the guards there dealt with them."

The three carts were now speeding at eighty miles per hour, as they were no longer hauling the weight of another five carts carrying obsidian and iron.

Thorn put away his bow and turned to the barrel on the cart.

As the milk flowed from the tap, he said, "Nether's gotten bad. We got Ender dragons flying around, ghasts attacking, Herobrine being all creepy."

Thorn looked up. His eyes followed something
quickly before he returned to Steve.

"I just saw him," he said, pointing as the world raced by.

Steve turned and looked. If he had been there, there was no way for Steve to tell.

"This is all his fault, I'm telling you," Thorn said.

Steve looked around. The obsidian hills, crimson trees, rivers and falls were all a blur.

"How much longer till we get to North Mine?"

"At this rate, an hour."

Steve nodded, and sat down.

The rattle of the links was almost drowned out by the roar of the carts barreling north.

Neither of them spoke for the rest of the journey.

An hour later, Thorn reduced power and the speedometer needle began to arc back as the speed dropped. From three kilometers away, Steve could see North Mine. There were about ten buildings and towers.

"Half of them are breakrooms," Thorn said. "This is one of Golden Gate's most important mines. Miners have to work long hours, but the council compensates with good food and lodging. I've wanted to transfer here, but the far west mine is understaffed as is."

The carts slowed as they turned from their track to another. It was crowded with other carts for as far as Steve could see.

Thorn's carts halted ahead of another line of carts.

A station crewman ran up to connect the links.

"Alright, last shipment!" He shouted.

The stationmaster greeted them as a great engine a few yards ahead of Thorn's cart began moving backwards.

Thorn and Steve walked out of the cart.

"Driver Thorn," the stationmaster greeted them.

"Stationmaster Axel," Thorn responded.

"What happened to the rest of the carts?"

"We were attacked by ghasts some eighty miles back. We lost five carts," Steve said.

"Who is this?" Axel asked, turning to Steve.

"A friend, his name is Steve." said Thorn. "Chief of Transportation said he could travel with me from Far West. He was just sightseeing. He's a colonizer, looking around. He's also been seeing some queer things with Herobrine, and the Ender dragon."

The stationmaster looked at Steve.

"Well, I guess if Henry signed you off... are you heading back to Golden Gate?"

The portal back to Golden Gate was rippling purple ahead of the great engine as it arrived at the cart, and the same crewman who had connected Thorn's carts to the others linked the engine to the line of carts.

"Not yet," Steve responded. "There's still some things I've got to take care of. Do you know anything about Herobrine?"

The stationmaster thought for a moment.

"Other than that he's weird, shows up everywhere, and leaves buildings and stuff behind, no. Why?"

"He tried to kill me. Yet he also warned me when my dog was being attacked by the Ender dragon."

The stationmaster looked at him.

"I'm sorry, Steve, I don't know much about him. But I don't think you should go checking something you shouldn't. This place is different. It is not the Overworld where things are straightforward."

"True," Steve said. "Seems that Herobrine actually lives here, some way from Far West."

"Oh?" Axel said. "Well, that's more reason not to mess with Herobrine. There are powers here that even the council doesn't understand."

Steve turned at the sound of the engine lurching forward, and the line of carts following, their links and cargo rattling.

The engine was no boiler-run vehicle. It was powered by redstone. There were pistons, but they were electrically powered. The engine produced no fumes as it chugged forward, headed for the portal.

A few moments later, it began to go through. First, the engine disappeared, then Thorn's cart, and then the rest. One by one they went through the portal, as those that had gone through already appeared before another portal, at the doorstep of Golden Gate.

"We did see him recently, though," Axel said.

Steve turned to see him.

"He left a ship, with guns. It's over there."

Steve looked to where he was pointing.

It hadn't looked like a ship from afar because there were no sails or masts to be seen. There were only the rockets, sitting dormant by the gunwales near the pilot's station.

The prow was a great cannon, and there were multiple swivel guns along the rails.

The ship had gun ports that hid other cannons.

"The council sent some people to check it out. It's powered by redstone. It's reinforced with Netherite, the guns are capable of demolishing castles, and the ship's hold already contains ammo."

Steve looked at Axel.

Netherite was especially strong, Steve knew.

Thorn didn't know what to say.

"A gunship? Why?"

"No clue. Our first worry was that there was TNT and other bomb material, but there was none of that. And there's no crew or any sign of a computer, so no one can control it remotely."

"Nothing dangerous can be trusted to not hurt others if there is someone who can just pop up wherever whenever," Steve said, angrily.

He looked at the ship again.

Its hull was oak and iron.

"The ship's heavily armed," Axel went on. "This thing's meant for battle."

"It's what this thing is meant to battle that worries me," Steve said. "And why would Herobrine leave something like this for us? Anyway, I'm going to head back to Far West. When's the return trip?"

"There'll be a train carrying workers to the mine leaving about half an hour from now."

Steve nodded.

"I'll be there," Thorn said. "I've got to go back to help with moving the rest of the shipments."

Steve nodded.

"Breakroom's that way," Axel pointed to the building a block away. It was a wooden thing, three stories high, with windows that allowed for a view of the mine, the tracks, and the portal.

"You go ahead," Thorn told Steve. "I've got to write my report."

Steve nodded and walked off the platform, headed for the breakroom, as Thorn crossed the tracks to the chiefs'
building.

Steve walked by one of the cobble roads with the other crews headed for the breakroom. Guards stood sentry at the buildings and he could hear the miners picking away at the earth as they walked.

Steve reached the breakroom a few moments before the track crews. The hall was cool and the white light was a welcome change from the red, gloomy aura of the Nether.

People were talking and laughing, just as they had been at Far West. Here, the drinks were water, milk, coffee, cocoa, and some others. There was food as well… steak, bread, and stew.

No one paid him any mind as Steve sat at a table.

A waiter arrived a moment later.

"What do you want?" the waiter asked.

"A cup of cocoa and a steak, please," Steve said.

The waiter hurried off.

He returned a minute later with a chilled tankard of cocoa.

"Thanks," Steve said.

He sipped.

The waiter disappeared.

Steve's tankard drained as his steak cooked somewhere beyond sight.

While he waited for Thorn and the food, he thought about what had happened, and wondered whether the fungi he'd planted were growing.

Then the door opened and Thorn appeared.

He walked towards the table.

"Thorn," Steve said, as he sat down, "what do you know about warped fungi? How long does it take to grow?"

"It'll be taller than a house soon enough," Thorn said.

The waiter arrived with Steve's steak.

"You?" He looked at Thorn.

"Steak as well. And cocoa."

The waiter hurried off again.

"Can you tell me everything you know about this new Nether?" Steve said.

"Well, the crimson trees and fungi are new. There's also some new mobs and stuff. If you want, you can still mine the ground. Light will keep everything away. You can find all kinds of things there, like Netherite."

Steve nodded.

He chewed a chunk of his steak and sipped his cocoa.

The waiter returned with Thorn's food and drink.

Just as Steve was about to drink the last of his drink, the door opened and a messenger appeared.

"All miners and staff of North Mine," he announced.

Everyone turned to listen.

"By decree of the Chiefs of the Mines, all transports will now be guarded by military convoys. The threats detected by our scouts and the attack suffered by Driver Thorn is proof that the Nether has grown dangerous. No one can travel unarmed and all transportation must be guarded."

Muttering swept through the crowd.

When no one said anything back to the messenger, he left.

Thorn looked at Steve.

"There's going to be a fight," he said. "I can feel it. Perhaps that gunship is actually going to help us."

Chapter 7: Convoy Attack

Less than half an hour later, Thorn and Steve were boarding one of the empty cart trains headed for Far West.

Ahead, there was a train populated by soldiers armed with enchanted weapons. Behind it, empty transport carts stretched for a mile long, and then there was another train of armed soldiers.

Thorn shook his head.

"Never thought there would be a time when torches and staying hidden weren't enough to fight the mobs."

"Me either," Steve said, sadly.

A few minutes later, the stationmaster ordered the trains to get moving. The first guard train started off.

Rattling away, Thorn engaged the redstone drive once there was ten feet between their train and the guard train.

A few moments, later, the second cart train started following, and then the third. Finally, the tenth train began to move while Thorn and the first set of soldiers were barreling away at fifty miles per hour.

Anyone looking from above would be able to see the column heading away from North Mine.

Silence hung on the convoy for the thirty minutes as the carts raced off, rattling, as their redstone engines roared.

Then a shrill cry split the air and Steve spun to see a group of ghasts hurtling toward them.

"Mobs!" A soldier shouted.

Arrows began flying from the carts at once as they raced by.

Thorn fired, as Steve stood ready to deflect a projectile.

Another piercing shriek made Steve wince.

The ghasts were keeping up with the carts. Arrows hissed through the air, and the ghast directly ahead of Steve launched a round of fire from three carts away.

The burning orb hurtled toward Steve as the cart roared on.

Steve struck it with his blade, and sent the fires rushing back to the ghast. It hit the mob, but the ghast didn't go down.

Another round of fire launched from one of the ghasts farther up.

One of the soldiers at once switched to his sword and struck the round before it hit the carts, sending it back to the ghast.

One out of the ten ghasts finally dropped away, amidst a hail of arrows.

Another shrill cry cracked the air, as Thorn peppered the ghast ahead of them with arrows and it launched another round of fire.

Steve couldn't let them hit. If they did, the cart would be derailed, the ones behind them would be harmed, and all the people they carried would be hurt.

He struck the burning orb.

It soared back toward the ghast, and the mob shrieked and fell away.

"One," he told Thorn.

Thorn turned and fired a series of arrows at another ghast. It went down two seconds later.

"One," he said.

The carts were now twenty-five percent of the way from North-North-West Mine, about half an hour from where Steve and Thorn had been attacked earlier.

The carts raced past an obsidian hill, the almost black blocks racing past and appearing as a blur.

Thorn and the rest of the drivers and the soldiers were loosing arrows at the ghasts, striking at rounds of fire with their swords, when another mob ahead of them launched a burning orb.

Steve deflected it and it flew back trailing smoke and flame, as Thorn loosed twenty arrows at the thing. Ten more, and the ghast fell away.

"Two," he said to Steve. "You may be young, kid, but that don't mean you're better."

Steve chuckled.

"Lava ahead!" One of the soldiers shouted.

Steve looked ahead and saw the pool of lava drawing near.

If they fell over that, they'd die, though they would just respawn at Golden Gate.

It would be quite troublesome.

"We gotta take them down before we reach the lava!" Steve shouted.

"Aye," Thorn said, loosing an arrow at another ghast.

Somewhere off the first guard train, a soldier deflected a round of fire, and the ghast that had launched it fell away when it was hit.

Before long, there was just three still attacking the column.

Thorn downed one with a hail of arrows, Steve sent of the other's rounds of fire hurtling back, and a soldier fired a barrage of arrows at the last one.

When the shrieks and the ghouls had fallen away, they were clear of the lava.

The next part of the journey elapsed with only the roar of the engines and the rattle of the wheels. Every soldier and driver remained alert, ready to fight off any mob that showed itself.

Steve was watching the rails rush past as a blur. There was

still an hour's distance till Far West, and though none of them would run out of ammo, they couldn't guarantee that they were going to be able to defeat another round of mobs. Ghasts weren't the only things to fear. For all they knew, there could be Wither Bosses, crafted by Herobrine, and a contingent of soldiers like this wouldn't be able to defeat two of them.

An hour went by before Thorn spoke.

"Nether's growing dark," he said. "And it's all because of that Herobrine fella. I swear, if I see him again, I'm going to kill him, or find a way to banish him."

Steve thought before he replied.

"I think we need to know the truth about him before we decide his fate."

Thorn looked angry.

"The truth?" He said. "Here's the truth. He's been causing trouble for all of us. Less than most of the buildings he leaves behind are some kind of trouble. Were it me deciding, I'd demolish that gunship. Ain't nothing there."

"Well, I still think we should try to talk to him first, and find out what's really going on."

Thorn looked out at the red sky.

"Well, then you gotta find him first."

The carts arrived at Far West before long. The first train of soldiers stopped ahead of Thorn's as he disengaged the redstone drive and engaged the brakes. The other trains stopped as well, and then the second train of soldiers.

Chief Henry was standing beside the stationmaster, eyeing the column.

He could tell they were restless.

"What happened?" Henry asked.

"Chief of the Mines said that all transports will be guarded from henceforth," Steve said. "We were attacked by an army of ten ghouls while traveling."

Henry and the stationmaster looked at each other. The stationmaster turned to forward the message as the soldiers and drivers began debarking.

"You alright?" Henry asked Steve and Thorn.

"Yeah," Steve said. "I've decided I'm going to look for Herobrine. I'm going to meet him. I'm not going to let him go, and I'm going to find out what is happening."

Thorn nodded.

"I'd end him as is," he said, "but I agree."

Henry considered it.

"Well, if you think you're able, then fine. I wish you good fortune, and would lend you soldiers if I could, but the mine must be defended."

Steve nodded.

"Thanks," he said. "I'll leave an hour from now."

Thorn and Steve walked to the break-room, the much simpler counterpart of North Mine's.

The hall was crowded with a different group of miners than the ones Steve had met earlier.

These folk seemed just as friendly though.

"Headquarters says all transports will be armed now," Thorn said as they walked to the bar.

The hall fell silent as the crowd looked at him.

"We were attacked by ghasts while traveling to North Mine, and while we were traveling back," Steve said. "The second time, we had soldiers with us, and there were ten ghasts. And Herobrine apparently left something at North Mine. A gunship, with rockets. Headquarters are unsure whether it's dangerous or not. They haven't found anything to prove it is, so nothing's been done yet."

Mutters swept through the hall.

"So Herobrine's been causing all our trouble," one of the

miners said. "What's headquarters going to do about him?"

"I'm going to look for him," Steve said.

The miners looked at him.

"I'm going to find him, I'm going to speak to him, and I'm going to find out the truth."

"But he's a bad guy," one of the miners protested. "It ain't safe."

"And don't forget," Thorn added, "that he tried to kill you."

"I still don't know anything for sure."

Steve ordered a steak and a tankard of coffee, while Thorn ordered stew and tea.

The hall returned to its chatter and talk before long, though the conversation now was about Herobrine and Steve going to look for him.

When Steve had cleaned his plate and drained his tankard, he said, "I'm going to leave after this, head back to my house and search along the way. I will find him."

Thorn looked at him sadly.

He nodded.

"Just be careful."

"I will."

Chapter 8: Wastelands & Adventurers

Steve left the mine by the same path he had walked to get there.

Lava was falling from a cliff a hundred blocks away and the sky was red, as always. The ground was cracked and sandy. Where there was heaps of clay, one step was enough for the ground to fall away to dust.

Steve kept walking till he began to feel hungry. Then he retrieved one of the steaks he had bought from Far West and scoffed it up.

He drank some of his milk as he walked, and felt refreshed.

About ten blocks away was an obsidian hill, purple and dark and gleaming, made darker still by the red sky.

He walked past.

Then he stopped.

He remembered what Thorn had told him, that the ground held many precious resources. He also wanted to know what mobs would spawn there.

He decided he would mine near his house.

Steve kept on walking. For hours he walked. He saw a few ghasts, but they were just suspended above the ground, asleep. The piglins he encountered did nothing to harm or stop him. All the skeletons along the way fell by his blade.

He reached his warped fungi plant five hours after leaving Far

West. It had grown some, into a green shrub.

Steve went on, following the trail of soul torches for the last leg of the journey.

Nothing about his house had changed. The soul torches still stood sentry outside, and he could see his portal back to Beaconlight.

He didn't need to get anything from the house, so he started mining as soon as he got there, about ten blocks from the door.

Block after block disappeared.

He cleared squares of four blocks as he tunneled below ground, lighting torches when it grew dark.

He had been mining for ten minutes when the light grew dim, and one of the blocks disappeared to reveal a sea of lava.

It was bright, and there was almost no ground, but a few blocks of stone.

He looked at one of them, narrowing his eyes.

Without thinking, hearing only the words, "Are you crazy?" he jumped.

Aiming for one of the blocks of stone, he landed and lost half a life.

The wall opposite him was dull stone. Almost everywhere was stone. Only the ground was lava.

He placed a stone block before him and walked to it from the stone block he stood on.

He built his way to the space from which the river of lava flowed as far as he could see.

Peering out, he saw the river of lava flowing from a cascading molten fall.

There was nothing there besides the lava but obsidian.

He turned back and headed to the stone block he had fallen to, picking up the other blocks as he went.

Reaching the original spot, he began building his way up, and was soon at his own mine. He sealed it off and climbed back to the surface.

There was his house, the soul torches, and the portal.

Disappointed, Steve decided he would try mining another time.

Now, he had to feed Sean, then start planning how to look for Herobrine.

He went to his portal, stepped through, and emerged amidst the green plains and sunshine of the Overworld.

Steve felt life return to him as he walked past his townsfolk and farms, to his house.

Sean was barking at the door, and Steve had never been happier to see him. He opened the door and petted him.

"Buddy!" He shouted. "How are you? Things good at Beaconlight? Good."

He fed him some of Far West's steaks and then pet him.

"Okay, I have to go again," Steve told him, "but I'll be back about three days from now."

He left by the same oak door.

"Mornin', Jack," he said to the cartographer.

"Mornin'," Jack muttered.

"Colonizer Steve, nice to see you. Where have you been?" the farm-caretaker said.

"The Nether," Steve replied. "Looking for some stuff."

"Oh. You be careful!"

Steve was almost sad to leave Beaconlight again, but he knew he had to. Something was happening, and Herobrine needed to be dealt with. So he stepped through the portal and returned to the Nether, the cracked earth, red sky, and the realm of mobs.

He walked to his house, and sat beside his crafting table.

He looked at his map of the Nether. There was the railroad he had traveled with Thorn, the ground he'd walked to get to Far

West, and North Mine. The lava river he'd crossed traveling to North Mine ran directly north-east. Obsidian ranges formed most of the map, with some spots designated with a sword as dangerous zones. Those areas didn't necessarily house worse mobs, just more of them, too much for one person to fight.

Steve didn't know if he could go there. He had slayed an Ender dragon, fought crowds of creepers, Endermen, skeletons, and zombies. He had fought ghasts and ghouls…but he'd always fought them alone, or no more than a few at a time. These dangerous plains usually meant that at least a hundred of each kind was there. If he died there, he'd lose his stuff there, and never be able to regain it.

"Does that mean I get someone crazy enough to follow me?" Steve asked himself.

No one from the mines would, and almost no one from Beaconlight. Golden Gate might have some people willing to, but Steve had no idea who.

Then he realized.

"Sam," he said.

Sam was also a colonizer, and he was the mayor of Gatepost, thirty thousand blocks from Golden Gate. He had a town to govern, but he could appoint someone to administer while he was away. Sam had always wanted to be an explorer. He'd spent his childhood exploring the mines near the city, and when he was enrolled to train as a colonizer, he would complete his homework to go mining.

Perhaps he'd changed now, Steve thought. Perhaps he was now more focused, more aware of his responsibilities. But he might not be.

He would be the only person who'd agree to join him.

So Steve rose, and left for his portal.

He got back to Beaconlight a few seconds later.

He walked to the Main Gate, where torches crackled. Fire was the guardian of all of things.

"Here, anyway," Steve thought as he left Beaconlight.

His spirits had been elevated by the green plains and hills, the blue sky, the sun, the animals, and the water. He pitied the miners who had to spend hours looking at the red sky and the molten falls.

Gatepost was a thousand blocks away.

He could see its great tower from five hundred blocks away, rising tall and proud.

The cobble road leading from Beaconlight to Gatepost was flanked by thistles and hedges, with great oak and pine trees looming beside them. The road to Golden Gate could be seen straight forward while this road branched off. There were a few farms along the way, managed by folk who preferred the simplicity of rural life but appreciated the safety the city supplied.

He hailed them as he walked past.

A hundred blocks from the Main Gate, nine hundred northwest of Beaconlight, he spotted the sentries who manned the barbican. They were meant more for the policing of the city than the guarding of it, and stood with their backs to him, following the fashion of Golden Gate. They carried no weapons. Should they spot a criminal, they would call him out and chase him. Honest folk would help.

The gates and oak doors were open, so Steve walked through, past the ring of torches.

The city was crowded.

Farmers sold their crops at the marketplace, and a smith forged swords nearby as carpenters crafted bows and arrows. Restaurants offered food and drink. The great tower, and the great keep, built after their counterparts in Golden Gate, rose like a stone giant wielding a club from which could be seen the entire city.

That was where Sam would be.

The main streets were cobblestone and the lesser roads were oak. Most of the buildings were made of pine and stone. Trees grew along the streets, along with orchards and shrubs. It was a green city, as Sam had declared it would be. Gatepost sought to counter its smoke emissions, so the green compensated for the smoke of armories and torches.

The air was much cleaner because of that. Also a great deal more nourishing than the air of the Nether.

Before long, Steve reached the doors of the great keep.

The two guards let him through, one of them going ahead of him to tell Colonizer Sam that Steve had arrived.

The stone steps and castle were a cold comparison to Steve's oak home. But Sam had always been one for contemporary style, as the world moved toward stones. Steve saw the use of stone, and had built stone structures at Beaconlight, but preferred oak and pine for his own home.

The climb saw them ascend two hundred steps, rising past other levels where Gatepost's administrators worked.

Those people would be able to govern for Sam while he was away, Steve was sure.

Gatepost had developed a great deal more, with much less time, than Beaconlight had. Steve had founded Beaconlight three years ago. The city was now half-farm, half-city. The city boasted a marketplace, armory, and the yearly tournaments for athletes that traveled Golden Gate's cities, with the final game happening at Golden Gate. Gatepost had only been established a year ago, and seemed twice as great.

"How many people are there here?" He asked the guard.

"About ten thousand," the guard said, happily.

Steve nodded.

Beaconlight only had two.

But Beaconlight would grow at Steve's pace, he decided.

They reached the oak doors of Sam's office five minutes later.

"Thank you," Steve told the guard as he turned to leave.

Steve opened the right panel.

Sam was sitting at his desk, sunlight shining through the windows.

The room was stone, but its furniture was oak and pine.

"Steve!" Sam greeted him happily, rising from his seat.

"Sam, it's good to see you," Steve said, hugging him.

"You too," Sam smiled. "How have you been?"

"Good. Beaconlight is well too, and I see Gatepost is."

"Aye," Sam said. "Our farms are growing well, and trade with the other colonies has helped significantly."

"I'd think so."

"Now," Sam said, walking to his seat. "Cocoa? Coffee? Milk? Tea?"

"Cocoa, please," Steve said.

Sam turned to the barrel of cocoa and poured two cups.

"Please, sit," Sam told him, as he handed him his drink.

The drink was chilled, and nicer to drink here than in the Nether.

"So, what brings you to Gatepost?" Sam asked, as he sat.

"I've been looking around the new Nether."

Sam's face turned serious.

"And?"

"I defeated an Ender dragon, and a mining transport I was traveling with was attacked twice by ghouls. The first time, one of their rounds of fire hit us and we lost most of the carts. Before the trip back from North Mine to Far West, the chiefs decreed that all transports would be armed. We were attacked by ten ghouls before twenty-five percent of the return trip was complete. Luckily, we defeated all of them. And then there's Herobrine, whom I hear was standing outside your office three weeks ago."

"Herobrine?" Sam leaned forward.

"Yeah."

"I didn't see him."

"Yeah, probably not. He left a pyramid with a portal near my house that I'd built close to my own portal. I went through the pyramid's and was transported to the Overworld, to some desert plain. There was a cavern guarded by a creeper. I slew it, then a spider, then I was looking around when Herobrine appeared. He talked about some war with the One, and how the eight gods are not the true god. Then he told me the Ender was attacking my house, where I'd left my dog. So I rushed back and slew the dragon. I sent Sean back to my home at Beaconlight. Then I went back, and started looking around. I found this obsidian castle. And there was a crafting table, furnace, books, potions, and Herobrine, and then dispensers that launched arrows at me. I ran. And now I think Herobrine's a bad guy but I'm not sure. Everyone else is certain.

I started growing warped fungi, then traveled to Far West. I met a driver there named Thorn, and he and I went to North Mine. It was during that trip we were attacked by three ghasts and lost most of the carts. When I got to North Mine, I saw how the carts are transported to Golden Gate, and left a half hour later with Thorn, other managers, and soldiers. While we were traveling back, we were attacked by ten ghasts. We defeated all of them.

We got back to Far West, and I left. When I got back to my house, I decided I'd try mining. I found a cavern of lava. Then I decided I'd look for you, to ask if you would be willing to help me find out what's going on. You were always going around, figuring out stuff like this," Steve concluded.

"Well, that was before, when I was not a colonizer and not confined to the office of a mayor."

"I'm sure you can appoint someone to administer while you're away."

"True. But I've changed Steve. I've got responsibilities now."

Steve thought for a moment.

"You're really going to let an opportunity to learn about the new Nether go in exchange for being mayor? Anyone can be mayor, but not anyone is able to be an adventurer."

"And what, I am?"

"Yeah."

Sam looked at him.

"I suppose I could go, appoint someone to look after things while I'm gone. Alright, fine."

Steve smiled.

"The first place we're going is the obsidian castle I told you about."

"Okay. Let me arm myself and call someone."

He pressed a button and the door opened.

"Aiden, could you send for Chief Hamud?"

The guard nodded and left.

Sam shut the door and rose.

He walked to his chests and donned golden armor, equipped an enchanted sword and bow and mining equipment.

"Gatepost might be better than Beaconlight," Steve said, "but you don't get much better than gold or enchanted."

"Thus, things will ultimately always be equal."

Chief Hamud appeared a moment later.

"Sir?" He said.

"I would like you to administer as mayor a while. I'm going to be leaving with my friend, Steve, for some time. I know you're capable."

"Why, thank you," Hamud said. "May I ask, where are you going?"

"To find Herobrine," Steve said. "Sam here is the most knowledgeable about this matter."

Hamud nodded.

"Well, be careful. Gatepost will still be flourishing

when you return."

Sam nodded.

"Now, Steve, let us go."

Steve turned and walked to the door first. He left the office, followed by Sam, and then they descended the hundred steps to ground level from the highest floor, near the spot where people could see the city through stone columns.

They met the guards who had greeted Steve a few minutes later.

"Sir," they saluted Sam and opened the doors.

The two walked out of the great stone castle. The streets were still crowded and alive with the sounds of commerce.

Wind sighed through the streets, rustling the trees and orchards.

"Clear the way for the mayor!" A guard shouted.

The crowd moved aside, hailing Sam.

Sam waved at them as they walked toward the Main Gate. They got there before long, and the people returned to their business once they'd left.

"We'll get to Beaconlight first," Steve said.

They started walking to get to the Golden Gate road.

"When was the last time you went to the Nether?"

"A month ago," Sam said. "It was almost the same as the old Nether, except for the fungi and crimson trees, and the zoglins and piglins."

"Did you notice anything odd?" Steve asked, his shoes crunching dry leaves.

"Not really. The mobs were about the same. But there were more ghasts. I saw Herobrine once."

Steve looked at him.

"What happened?"

"He was standing by an obsidian hill. Then he crafted the

same portal pyramid you talked about and left."

"Did you go through?"

"I did. But I didn't find a desert. I found green plains and a town. But he told me of the town being attacked by raiders, of it burning. I ran back through the portal. I haven't told anyone what happened."

"That was no dream of the future," Steve said. "I was told that an Ender dragon was attacking my house. And it was happening. What you heard was happening when he told you."

Sam's eyes widened.

"What is going on?" He said.

"I don't know," Steve said. "But Herobrine is connected somehow. And the new Nether as well. We need to find out what both are about."

They reached Beaconlight an hour later.

"Golden," Sam said when he spotted the oaken citadel, the farms, the pine and stone buildings. It was a tenth of the size of Gatepost.

"Regal, like Gatepost."

"Yeah, yeah, quit your boasting. Beaconlight's not as grand as Gatepost, but we have an important role as well. Our lighthouse signals safe harbor and helps ships navigate through storms and darkness, and it offers a point to follow for wandering people looking for a home. Creepers and zombies have caused trouble for Golden Gate's borderlands, so there has been a great deal of displaced people recently. That's another thing we'll have to solve."

Steve and Sam walked past the ring of torches.

The cobble road was flanked by guard barracks, houses, stables, farms, and other buildings. The marketplace
was somewhere ahead, and not as crowded as Gatepost's.

"We're a much saner people than yours," Steve said.

"Sadly, I must agree," Sam said.

"Colonizer Sam!" A voice cried.

They turned.

A guard was hailing from beside one of the torches.

"Sir," Sam said.

"It's an honor to meet you, Colonizer," the guard said. "What brings you to Beaconlight?"

"Some diplomatic talks," he said. "Perhaps your town and Gatepost will merge."

Steve tsked.

"Well, that would be splendid," the guard said.

Sam turned.

Steve was glaring at him.

"Seems your people don't like your town too much."

"He isn't my people," Steve said. "He's from Gatepost."

"What?"

"Yup."

Sam's look was surprise.

Steve smiled.

"That's right. Someone from your town wanted to leave for something better. He'll appreciate this town before long. Most of those who emigrated from Gatepost already have."

Sam did not respond, upset that people had left his town for Beaconlight.

They got to the portal before long, but Steve stopped and ran to his house to see Sean.

Sean barked at Sam when he saw him.

"Go on, feed him. Looks like he likes you."

Sam fed him a chunk of meat.

Sean ate it and barked again. He looked as if he were smiling.

Sam petted him.

"He's a nice dog," he said.

"Yes, he is. I adopted him a few days after settling here. He's been my friend since then."

They returned to the portal a minute later.

"Ready?" Steve said, as they stood before the shifting Golden Gate.

"Ready."

They stepped through.

Chapter 9: Obsidian Battlements

They emerged from the portal and went to the obsidian range.

Sam saw Steve's house.

"Good base," Sam remarked.

"It's just a simple house. I store some stuff there, and craft and forge stuff. This is where I slew the Ender dragon."

"That's impressive," Sam said.

They walked down to the house.

"So, here's the map," Steve said, holding it out. "If you want, we could either go to that obsidian castle, or we could check one of the dangerous zones. We'd probably find Herobrine at both."

"I say we go to the castle first."

"Alright."

Steve equipped his enchanted blade.

"Let's go."

They started walking west. About half an hour later, Sam spotted some gray blocks.

"Look at that," Sam said. "That's no ordinary stone. This is Netherite."

Steve looked at him.

"Netherite." Sam walked up to the thing. "Stronger than diamond. There used to be a great deal of it here, but the piglins mined it all. What's left is just a fraction. Most of the Netherite left is far below ground. A lot of the mines don't even get to it."

"I'm going to forge some armor with it."

"Wise. And a building built of Netherite wouldn't fall to anything, maybe to a wither, but even then, not really."

Steve mined a few blocks with his enchanted pickax. Netherite seemed to be stronger than any material Steve had mined before. It consumed a chunk of his pickax's health and a great deal more of his time by the time he had mined it.

"Better be worth it," he told Sam.

"It will be."

He placed a furnace before him.

"Forge some armor."

Steve walked up to it and combined the Netherite blocks to forge some plate armor.

A few minutes later, he put the armor on, but kept his golden helm to keep the piglins away.

He couldn't feel any difference, but Sam promised him his new armor would be useful when fighting.

"I suggest you rebuild your house with Netherite as well," Sam said, as he forged his own armor.

"I'll consider it," Steve said. "But for me to get enough, I'll need a great deal of equipment. Perhaps when this whole mess is figured out, I'll start mining."

They continued walking west. As they walked by an obsidian hill, Sam spotted something roaming ahead.

"Stop," he said.

He pointed at the thing. A tusked boar was walking some thirty blocks away.

"That's a hoglin," he said. "Best not go near those things."

Steve looked at the thing. It looked fearsome, but he had fought an Ender dragon.

"Those things can hurt more than you think," Sam said. "We

should just get past him."

Steve knew that Sam was an authority about things like this, so he decided he would trust him.

"Fine," he said. "We circle round."

So they walked on, quiet as they could be. When the hoglin walked away from them, they walked forward. When it stopped, they stopped. When it turned around, they doubled-back. Before long, they were clear.

"Don't fight one of those unless you have to," Sam said when they were a hundred blocks away from the creature.

Steve nodded.

They continued walking, past obsidian hills, crimson trees and warped fungi, and cavernous spaces that Sam said would contain Netherite.

Before long, they spied the obsidian towers and wall of the castle Steve had seen.

"Be careful," Steve said. "Though I guess our Netherite armor won't let any of the arrows harm us."

"Exactly."

With swords drawn, they approached the arch.

The torches were burning, and the obsidian blocks reflected their glow. But this time, the eerie silence, the dark obsidian, and the red sky, only made the fire seem more disconcerting than familiar.

They walked through the arch.

There was the crafting table, books, potions, and furnace. There were the dispensers as well, but no Herobrine.

"Where's that idiot?" Sam said.

"I don't know, but keep a lookout. And careful where you step. It was the pressure plate by the dispensers that triggered them. Don't go stepping on any more."

They walked across to the potions, watching the ground as they went.

They reached the table just as Herobrine appeared by the dispensers.

"Don't you dare," Sam said, aiming his bow at him.

Steve watched the silent figure.

His eyes moved, but nothing else.

"Who are you?"

"A friend," he responded, and stepped on the pressure plate.

"Steve!" Sam shouted, as arrows began flying from the dispensers. They rattled off their Netherite armor as they ran from the castle.

Steve and Sam kept running, running until they were at least a mile from the fortress.

"What the hell is he talking about? How is he a friend?" Sam said, angrily.

"He's got to be lying, but I don't understand," Steve answered. "And he knows our armor protects us, yet he still fires."

"So?"

"Maybe he doesn't mean to harm us, and is only keeping an act."

"Really?"

Sam's look was condescending.

"It's a possibility. Because he's really done nothing but help us."

Sam could see it, Steve knew.

There was a great deal of proof. When Sean was being attacked by the Ender dragon, Herobrine had warned him. When a town was being attacked, he warned Sam. Plus, no one would fire arrows at people with Netherite armor on.

"So you're saying if we stroll back there without armor, he won't fire at us."

Steve shook his head.

"I don't know."

"You sound crazy, Steve."

"I know, but we cannot disregard the possibility."

Sam didn't respond.

A moment went by.

"You alright?" Sam asked.

"Yeah. You?" Steve replied.

"Good. I think we should go to one of the dangerous spots. We have armor and we have weapons. We can fight. And there'd probably be stuff worth getting there. We can trade with piglins as well. We're wearing some golden armor, so they won't attack us."

"Alright," Steve said.

The closest dangerous spot was five hundred blocks northwest.

The path was cracked earth, and instead of the trees that lined the streets of Gatepost, Golden Gate, and the green cities, there were obsidian hills and molten lakes.

A hundred blocks from the dangerous zone, they spotted the mobs. Piglins, hoglins, zoglins, zombies, skeletons, ghasts, ghouls, withers. There were houses of Netherite, and no torches amongst the area the mobs occupied.

"You sure we can make it through that?" Steve asked.

"Yeah. Just keep fighting."

Steve nodded.

"If I don't make it out, you're gonna get my stuff back."

Sam laughed.

"Deal."

With his sword and shield before him, Steve started ahead first.

Sam followed with his bow.

It was a scene of deafening silence. Even the mobs remained quiet.

Then Sam fired an arrow and it sailed through the air, hitting one of the hoglins.

It shrieked, and then the mob saw them.

Shouting, Steve ran forward slashing at a skeleton with his sword as Sam's infinibow rained arrows.

The skeleton disappeared in a cloud of smoke as Steve turned to strike a wither. A skeleton fell beside him amidst a hail of arrows.

The zoglin fell moments later, and the ground around Steve was clear. But the withers and ghasts were racing toward them.

Sam rushed to join the fight with his blade, slashing at skeletons and withers.

A hoglin charged at Steve.

Steve held his shield before him, watching the mob race toward him.

When it was just a block away, Steve lunged with his sword and struck the beast. The hoglin blinked red, then attacked him.

Steve jumped back, then slashed. Again, it blinked red.

Sam cut down another skeleton when Steve struck the hoglin for the tenth time.

It didn't look like the beast would fall anytime soon.

He broke off and lunged at a skeleton. It a few moments later.

Then a round of fire from one of the ghasts crashed beside him, and a crater sprouted. Steve ran from the crater as another formed beside him.

Steve saw a round of fire racing towards Sam as he battled a skeleton.

"Sam, watch out!" He shouted.

Sam spun and saw the projectile. He deflected it, and sent the flaming orb back to the ghast. It struck the mob, and the wither disappeared in smoke.

"Nice!" Steve said, as he turned to defeat a skeleton.

Sam cut through the mobs' ranks with his blade, felling

skeletons and withers, running from hoglins when they attacked, and dodging wither-fire as Steve deflected what he could.

Craters dotted the ground where their ammunition had landed. The cracked earth was a crawling plain of mobs from the red world, with two from the green world also sweeping through. The men's Netherite armor guarded them well from the blades and arrows of the enemy.

One of the ghasts glided by an obsidian hill.

Steve darted for it, cutting down mobs as he went.

As he reached the hill, he stormed the steps and ran for the wither.

A chunk of fire crashed beside him, breaking off a chunk of obsidian.

Steve kept running.

Then, two blocks from the wither, he launched at it from the hill.

He struck the mob with his sword and it shrieked before falling away, and Steve fell the fifty blocks to the ground.

Landing with no lives lost, he slew a skeleton. Now the crowd of mobs had successfully been reduced to fifty.

Before long, the piglins were the last ones remaining. They did not want to attack because of their golden armor.

Steve and Sam slew the withers and the hoglins, but the fight had consumed a great deal of their health. They replenished with food.

"That was awesome," Steve told Sam as they stood amidst the clear field.

"Have you fought a battle like that before?"

"No. And I'm surprised I'm still alive!"

"I thought the withers would be difficult, but after defeating an Ender dragon, I think withers are simple."

"That's the spirit," Sam said. "Now, these piglins, we could trade with them for more Netherite."

"Sure."

They walked up to a group of piglins.

Steve still felt chilled by their appearance. They were walking humanoid pigs.

The group was willing to trade gold ingots for Netherite. Sam and Steve completed the trade, then the piglins placed twenty blocks of Netherite before Steve.

"Thanks," Steve said, collecting the Netherite. "Now let's get away from these things."

They left the dangerous spot.

But just as they were walking away from its borders, Sam spotted Herobrine, standing by a hill of obsidian.

"What's he doing?" He asked.

"I don't know," Steve said. "Perhaps we should talk to him. If he attacks us, we can fight. But we cannot kill him."

Sam nodded, reluctantly.

They walked towards Herobrine, while he just remained there, looking.

When they were twenty blocks away, Steve hailed him.

"What are you doing?"

"You must figure that out yourself," Herobrine answered. "And I pray you never have to, and that his plan will be completed before you can."

Then he disappeared.

"He normally doesn't talk," Sam said.

"So?"

"He *never* does."

"Doesn't mean he can't."

Sam looked at him.

"Right."

"Let's head back to the house. We can rebuild it."

Sam nodded, and they started walking. A half hour later, while they were walking past a pile of obsidian, they heard the shrill cry of an Ender dragon. They spun around to see it racing toward them.

How could there be more than one Ender dragon, Steve thought.

Sam at once equipped his bow and fired a series of arrows at the beast while Steve stood ready to strike.

The dragon swooped low, and fired a round of flame from its jaws.

Sam and Steve jumped aside as it crashed down and the ground sprouted a crater of stone and earth.

"Keep firing!" Steve shouted, and Sam launched another hail of arrows at the black dragon, its purple eyes glowing.

Another lance of flame escaped its jaws. It tore up the ground and Steve waited for an opportunity to strike it.

There were no obsidian hills when he needed them, nowhere for him to climb so that he could reach the beast.

The dragon blinked red with every arrow that struck it, as it circled, breathing fire.

An eternity went by before the beast flew low enough for Steve to strike its wing.

The dragon shrieked and spun to launch fire, but Steve jumped aside.

The dragon flew past just as the round of fire crashed, and Steve struck it again.

The beast finally fell hours later. Sam and Steve had lost almost no lives.

"Good fight," Steve said.

"Aye."

"Now, let's get back to the house."

They started walking again, reaching the stone-and-oak

structure about twenty minutes later.

"Good defense," Sam remarked. "Rebuild your house with Netherite and it'll be better."

Steve started removing the blocks from the right wall and replaced them with Netherite. He only had twenty-three, so he could only rebuild half of the right wall and half of the wall where the iron door was.

"We'll get some more," Steve said. "For now, we've got to figure out what happened, and then go out again. Herobrine said he hopes we'd never have to understand. What did he mean by that?"

"Well, he just doesn't want anyone causing trouble."

Steve thought for a moment.

"You're probably right. So where do we go next?"

"I got some dynamite," Sam said. "Perhaps we could go attack his castle.

Steve looked surprised.

"Sam, that is wrong."

"He's our enemy. Fighting him is not wrong."

"What if he's actually our friend?"

"You really believe that? You've never fought a war, have you? Gatepost has been attacked by raiders more than we can care to count. Called the War of the Outlaws. It's still happening. Once, we defeated this army, and about ten of them decided to join us. We accepted them, and freed them of their chains. They were allowed to roam the castle, but not the city. They told us everything about their tribe. And then one day, the Great Tower collapsed."

Steve remembered the news, but he'd only head a fraction of it, and different sources told different tales.

"And the raiders attacked. They attacked from the streets of the city and from the surrounding fields. They were let through the gates, and the fight was costly. The lives lost returned eventually, but a great part of the city had fallen. The Great Tower was gone, a part of the keep as well. The marketplace burned. All chests had been looted and the surrounding fields cleared. Golden Gate managed to supply us till we could fend for ourselves again."

Steve could hear his pain.

"We trusted those who claim to be friends before, and we paid dearly for that."

He turned and walked off.

Steve thought about what he said.

Raiders were the Overworld's greatest threat, and they had caused a huge amount of damage. Herobrine was no raider, and the mobs of this red world were no bandits. If Herobrine was plotting something dark, it needed to be stopped. It would be best to see him as an enemy. There was more cause for that than for thinking him a friend. The red world had grown worse since he started appearing here. New mobs, new powers. Something fallen was rising.

Steve ran to rejoin Sam.

"Okay," he said. "We attack."

Sam looked at him, and nodded.

They reached the castle before long, with no sun to tell the time, only the same crimson sky.

"I'll start placing the dynamite. Keep a look out for Herobrine or anything else."

"Okay," Steve said.

With his blade ready, he remained watchful as Sam placed dynamite along Herobrine's defenses. He built towers of stone to climb up to the merlons, where he placed more blocks of dynamite. Before long, there were fifty blocks of dynamite, all ready to demolish the wall and chunks of the towers.

"Get back," Sam told Steve.

Steve ran from the archway as Sam lit one of the dynamite blocks.

Then Sam ran too, and they were a hundred blocks away

when the dynamite went off. The rest of the blocks went off one by one, sending clouds of smoke billowing out as the obsidian blocks disintegrated and disappeared.

The roar of the dynamite echoed through the air, and Steve saw what was left as the smoke cleared. Blocks jutted out from where the obsidian wall still stood. Chunks of the watchtowers had fallen away, leaving the rest floating above the ruined parapets.

A great part of the ground had been deformed. A trench of soul sand and earth ran along where the wall had been.

Beyond that, not much damage had been dealt to where Herobrine stored his equipment.

They couldn't see Herobrine anywhere.

Steve started walking first, toward the castle grounds, followed by Sam.

"I'm going to place charges at the dispensers," Sam said.

He walked off to where the line of dispensers was and placed the dynamite, while Steve remained watchful.

Sam searched everywhere first, looking beyond where the arch used to be to the rest of the castle grounds. There was nothing.

"Okay," Sam said.

They stepped back as the dynamite went off. The dispensers disappeared amidst the cloud of smoke, and what was left was a ruin. The mechanics of the dispensers could be seen and their stores of arrows as well.

They wouldn't be firing any time soon.

"Thought he'd show up," Sam said.

"He will. Though we should perhaps fear how he will retaliate for his house being demolished."

All of a sudden, both their eyes glowed bright, and they staggered back.

They saw glimpses, glimpses of a hidden figure, standing before a computer block. They could see the soul block, and the three wither heads.

Then the vision morphed, and they saw a one-hundred headed wither sweeping through the sky, its great eyes scouring the ground with beams of light, rounds of fire launching from its jaws. They saw the great colonies of Golden Gate fall away, the fields turned to wastelands, and Golden Gate reduced to craters.

Steve and Sam fell back, weakened.

"What was that?" Sam said.

Steve's look was grim.

"That was a Wither, but not like any that's ever been seen."

Chapter 10: War Brewing

"We've got to warn them!" Sam said.

"We'll get back to Beaconlight. Tell the folks there, then make for Golden Gate. Once Golden Gate knows, the rest of the kingdom will know, and we can help the rural folk. Though this isn't going to stop the person who's making the Wither."

"That can be figured out later."

They turned and ran from the castle.

Fear energized their steps as they raced back to the portal.

They got there minutes later, and ran through.

Beaconlight greeted them as they appeared at the portal.

"Prepare to abandon the city!" Steve shouted. "A Wither attack is imminent."

Mutters erupted and the people looked confused.

"Don't panic! Everything will be fine! But you need to leave. Make for Golden Gate at once!"

The people started running back to their homes to pack their things while Steve ran toward his house.

Sean was barking at the door.

"Sean, we gotta go," he told him, walking him out.

The streets were chaotic as people ran past each other, most already carrying their stuff and running with their families.

They started walking up the Beaconroad as Steve and Sam

reached them.

"We warn the council," Steve said. "We create a plan, and then we stop this before it gets any worse."

Sam nodded.

They reached the gates of Golden Gate an hour later.

"We must speak with the council at once," Sam said to the guards, who eyed the frantic crowd with surprise.

"Are you certain?" King Jesse asked.

"Unfortunately," Steve replied. "Sam and I saw it both. It could be a trick, but we cannot take that risk."

"Perhaps it's a trap," the Lord of the Armies said. "What if the enemy is preparing something worse, and is trying to distract us?"

"It's a possibility," Steve said, "but we cannot take that risk. Evacuate the kingdom. We can go to North's End. And we should help as many of the locals as we can. Withers are not mobs we can easily fight. We can't run forever, but it's the best option now. These visions, they aren't visions of the future. They are of the present. This one, I think, contained one of the future as well, but there's a good chance that the Wither has already been created. I request soldiers to find it and slay it."

"I support him," Sam said.

The council members looked at them.

"Fine," the king said. "Steve and Sam here are the best colonizers of the kingdom, and brighter than some. If they're saying this, we shouldn't doubt them. Now get ready. Prepare to abandon the city."

The king's orders were forwarded to the city guard and army.

"Make for the northern gate!" The guards shouted at the people. "Pack only what is necessary. We must be able to travel with haste!"

Messengers were sent to the other cities, and Steve stood

before the formation of soldiers King Jesse had transferred to him. They had orders to hunt the wither and slay it.

The one hundred soldiers who stood before him were the kingdom's best.

Armed with bows and swords, and boasting diamond armor, they looked at their temporary captain.

"Soldiers of Golden Gate! A thousand years ago, the cities of this world banded together to fight a group of Withers released by Osgoth, a terrible energy that sought to turn our green fields to waste and our blue skies to smoke, in order to rule a desolate land populated by monsters and foul creatures.

"But we defeated those withers, and Osgoth. And the world endured. But a new power is rising, one perhaps just as bad or worse than Osgoth. Colonizer Sam and I have seen it. Someone is gathering the forces of darkness. Somewhere, they are crafting a Wither unlike any that has ever been. We only saw one, but there could be more.

The king has ordered all of Golden Gate to make for North's End and for us to help the locals as much as we can. We are to find what Wither there may be and slay it, and to find and capture the one who crafted it.

Will we yield?"

"No," they chanted back.

"Will we spare nothing to secure the safety of our people and our world?"

"Yes."

"Will you fight with me?"

"Yes!"

"Then let us depart. Our first destination is the Nether. Beware, my friends, for the Nether has changed. It is hostile as it always was, but worse. Worse mobs dwell there. Dragons and ghasts rule the skies and the lands are crawling with mobs. Always be on guard. Now, march, for you shall be heroes!"

The soldiers turned and began marching toward the portal that connected the city to the abandoned colony that was left amidst the wastelands.

Steve and Sam ran ahead and marched with them to the portal.

"At least he had imagination," Steve had said, when they decided to go there.

They walked through the portal and emerged amidst the ruins of the colony.

There was the uncompleted great stone keep, dark, with no torches, the marketplace, abandoned, and the desolate streets.

The first rank of soldiers arrived just then, and Steve and Sam moved forward to let the army march through the portal.

The ruins of a failed colony were too difficult to look upon, especially now. It signaled only loss, and doom.

But the soldiers paid it no mind.

"There was something I saw when we saw the Wither," Steve said. "Whoever the person crafting it is, they are here. And something tells me they are just north-west of here. But to get there, we'll have to get past an obsidian wall that rises two thousand blocks, with nothing jutting out for us to climb. We'll have to either get through it, or build structures to climb it. But we need to get to the other side."

"We can do it," a soldier said. "Some of us are combat engineers and combat builders. We'll either build you a way across, or get us through."

Steve nodded.

"Alright, let's get going. Just be aware, one of the dangerous zones is a thousand blocks west of here. We'll be going there. But we'll get through easily enough."

For an hour they marched West, going past obsidian hills, lava lakes, and a few piglins, who didn't attack.

Another hour went by, and they stood before the dangerous zone.

They spotted hoglins, piglins, Withers, ghasts, zoglins and skeletons.

The army halted a hundred blocks away, still beyond detection.

"Okay," Steve said. "We have to get through this. Sam and I defeated a dangerous zone before, and we've slain Ender dragons. You lot will do better and cut them down in less than an hour. Now charge."

The soldiers shouted and rushed forward, brandishing their swords.

Sam and Steve ran as well, as the roar of a hundred and two thundering towards their enemy echoed across the plain.

Then the shrill shrieks of the ghasts almost made the soldiers stop, but they kept running.

Their swords cut down the first line of skeletons as their shields guarded them from the arrows the skeletons located further back fired at them.

A round of fire from a ghast crashed amidst the formation, but the soldiers darted aside, and slew another mob as another round of fire crashed.

Steve jumped aside, and then something hit him. He almost fell, but he caught himself.

Around him, the battle had warped to be a shapeless, chaotic whirlwind of light and dark.

Shouts were shrieks, light was black, and darkness was white.

He tried to see how many lives he had. And he couldn't.

"Wither effect," he managed to say.

He decided he had to fight, but he couldn't.

He searched his stuff for the milk he had packed and drank it at once.

Then, a detonation cracked the ground around him as his vision returned.

One by one, the din of battle reached his ears again, as well as his sight.

A Wither was battling one Golden Gate soldier and Steve ran towards it.

He struck it thrice and it went up as smoke. He collected the points and moved on.

A ghast was firing a series of burning orbs at some of the soldiers, their red eyes glowing.

The ground was dotted with craters. Soldiers were battling hostile mobs, and Sam was fighing a hoglin.

Steve saw a zoglin charging toward him.

He waited, poised to dart aside, as the beast ran toward him, mindless.

When it reached him, Steve dodged, and struck the beast. Again he struck, then ten more times, and it was gone.

He felt pain stab through him then as an arrow hit him, and he turned to see a skeleton firing at him.

He ran toward it, shield before him. The oak absorbed the arrows as he reached the mob and slashed.

A few moments later, the skeleton disappeared.

The ghasts were falling one by one as the soldiers deflected their rounds of fire. The withers fell, but not before a few soldiers also did.

Finally, after an hour, the mobs were gone, and ninety soldiers regrouped.

"They will rejoin us shortly," Steve said. "Get their things. When they're with us, they'll get them back."

They marched on, headed for the obsidian castle, and arrived a half hour later.

"Bless the Builder," Chief Engineer Wallis said when he saw

the ruins of the obsidian castle, and the wall of obsidian that sealed off the rest of the west. "We'll use some dynamite to scope the barrier, then we'll decide how to get through."

Steve nodded.

The soldiers decided to set up camp by the ruins of the castle, away from the line of craters.

The soldiers drank milk and ate, while the Builders started placing dynamite.

Steve and Sam watched from afar.

Steve drank some milk and ate some stew.

"Fight was worse than last time," he told Sam. "Got hit by a Wither skeleton. Horrible feeling, and a horrible way to go."

"I can imagine."

"That super Wither," Sam continued, "it's not like any Wither. Whoever built this means to level cities. The computer block, I'm guessing, is to combine multiple Withers. The Wither we saw had ninety-nine heads, which means thirty-three wither bosses combined. That thing will decimate the world before we can run."

His tone was despairing.

"Do not lose hope," Steve told him. "Nothing has really happened yet. We could stop this before anything major does."

Sam nodded.

"Clear the area! Stand back fifty blocks!" Wallis shouted.

Some of the soldiers at the limits of the camp ran away, and then the first dynamite block was lit.

It went off just as the engineer who had ignited the fuse reached the distance Wallis had specified.

It triggered the other blocks, and when the smoke cleared, they saw a great cavern had been carved out of the mountain, with no end.

Wallis walked up to them.

"We could either keep using the dynamite to get through, or

we could build towers to get up."

Steve considered.

"Which will take less time?"

"The towers, sir."

"Then build them."

The chief nodded and turned to walk away.

Construction began at once. Three wooden towers rose hundreds of blocks high. The end of the obsidian cliff could not be seen, and soon, the towers disappeared as well.

A half hour later, the builders returned, and Wallis reported that the towers were complete.

"Prepare for the climb!" Steve addressed the army. "It's a thirty minute climb from here to the cliff. We may be attacked while ascending. Though chances are we won't. Whatever we find when we get to the top, do not be afraid. Our ancestors fought something like this, and defeated it. We can too."

The soldiers cheered.

"Begin the climb!"

Steve and Sam marched through the oaken door and began ascending the steps, followed by five soldiers at a time.

One of the soldiers began playing a song on his harp as they ascended.

Sky Giants, it was called.

"Giants of the sky, we call to learn to fly," he sang.

Others picked up the tune, and Steve listened as they climbed, almost feeling sad.

They reached the final level of the tower half an hour later, silent.

The doors at the highest levels were already open.

Silently, Steve marched out first.

The cliff grounds were obsidian, and that was all he could see for dozens of blocks before the rest was obscured by fog.

The sky was red, as usual, and other than soldiers filing out from the towers, there was nothing to be seen.

Sam followed, then the fighters.

"Tread carefully," Steve said. "There might be traps around here."

The army glided silently, treading lightly as they traversed the dark and rippling obsidian, which looked quite like a frozen sea.

They reached the fog soon. It was so heavy they couldn't really see each other, except for the silhouettes of their shields and weapons.

Still, everyone kept formation and made sure no one strayed from the path they walked.

Then they caught a glimpse of something beyond the fog bank. A red sky.

Steve walked toward it.

The fog grew clearer as they went. Steve could once again see Sam marching with his sword, and the soldiers with their blades and bows.

They were still walking on obsidian ground, and they could see a shear drop where the cliff ended. The cliff was square, and when Steve reached it, he saw it dropped fifty blocks.

There he saw the supreme Wither. There were a hundred Wither heads perched on several jutting out sections of T-formations comprised of soul sand.

It was a form that occupied most of the clearing.

Sam had no words. The soldiers muttered something, but all eyes were locked on the sight before them.

At the center of the giant wither was a computer block. Its lights were blinking.

"What is this?" Sam said.

"This thing is worse than any Wither boss, or any mob of nature. It has been enhanced. Its destructive capability is untold,"

Steve said.

Steve eyed the monster, his heart cold.

"Let's go to it," he said. "We could place dynamite and demolish it before its brought to life."

"I fear you might be too late," a voice echoed from the clearing.

The army bristled and they looked around, searching for the source of the voice.

Sam was searching too.

"Who are you?" Steve shouted.

The army settled when they heard Steve.

"I am he who will free this world," the voice responded.

"Free it from what?"

"From you. All of you. You have strayed from the path set by the gods. They do not appreciate people who oppose them."

"The gods respect our beliefs."

Steve still couldn't find the voice.

"The gods created this world, crafted the first island, crafted the first man. Do you think you are born? No," he laughed, "you are crafted. All of you are crafted. For thousands of years, the gods did not let you think, you had no free will. But, when things had fared as well as they did, they thought they could allow you free will. And what do you do? Stray from his path, conjure other religions."

"That is called being alive," Steve said.

"That is called madness," he snapped back, still hidden. "A madness that will be stopped. This storm will be unleashed. You will either change before the end, or suffer the consequences."

Sam was mad with anger.

"You know what?" Sam said. "We're stubborn."

"So be it."

He stepped forth from the shadows.

He was cloaked, so his face was hidden. He boasted golden

armor and was equipped with a shield and sword.

And beside him, was Herobrine.

Steve replaced his blade with Netherite.

He climbed up the blocks of soul sand and walked toward the computer block.

An archer trained his arrow.

"Don't," Steve said, as the stranger built a shell of Netherite to hide the computer.

Then he returned to the ground, and retrieved a wither head.

"This is the last one required to awaken the beast. I suggest you mend your ways."

The stranger added the wither head to the maze of those already there.

Then they heard a roar, and the earth cracking.

The monster began to move and twist. Herobrine and the one Herobrine had called the One were gone, but the wither remained, its blank eyes staring at the soldiers as it rose.

Steve eyed the rising mob.

"Steve?" Sam said.

"Run."

They turned and ran for the towers.

"Run!" Sam shouted.

The army retreated.

The Wither roared, a low and high shriek that split the air and set their heads to ringing.

Through the fog they ran, when rounds of fire began to fly from the wither.

It rained on the ground and formed craters amidst the obsidian.

Soldiers were shouting and running chaotically towards the towers.

They reached them a moment later and began the descent,

racing from the highest level.

Steve and Sam led the way by the first tower. As they climbed, they heard the roars of the wither and the breaking of earth as the wither bombarded the cliff.

As Steve and Sam thundered towards the ground, a round of fire hit the oaken planks and the tower almost fell.

Oak and obsidian flew out as a crater sprouted at the side of the cliff. Steve, Sam, and the soldiers who were running down looked up to see their compatriots at the rest of the tower ten blocks above.

"They can jump," Steve said.

He turned to run again, followed by the rest of the soldiers. The ones trapped beyond the crater dropped from the second half of the tower.

The wither was circling around the three towers, its eyes now glowing red, rounds of fire spraying from its jaws.

The cliff side was erupting with more craters as the fire hit, and before long, Steve was running out of the tower, along with Sam and the rest of the soldiers.

The rest of the army was pouring out from the second and third towers as well.

The Wither was a giant beast, casting a shadow with an area half of Beaconlight's.

Its red eyes glowed greater than a ghast's, and fire streamed from its mouth.

Clouds of smoke and dust erupted as the ground cracked and broke.

Steve was running when he saw a group of soldiers hit by a round of fire. Some others tried to fire at the beast with arrows, but they caused no damage.

"Run to the city!" He shouted.

A half hour later, with the Supreme Wither leaving a trail of cratered earth and soul sand, they reached the abandoned city, and the portal.

Steve ran through, followed by Sam, and the rest of the army.

The last soldier went beyond the reach of the Wither just as a round of fire crashed beside the portal.

Steve landed with his head ringing.

The sky was clear, and the air was cool, with green trees dotting the land, and birds squawking.

Steve felt refreshed at once.

Sam was beside him, looking around, as the soldiers stood amidst the field, drinking milk to regain their strength.

"This is isn't what we signed up for," one of them said.

"You signed up to help your people," Sam responded at once. "And defeating that Wither will help your people. We don't die, not truly, but do you really want us to live by running, always staying away from this threat that cannot be escaped? Sooner or later, that thing is going to leave the Nether, and we're going to have to stop it before that."

"We'll get back to Golden Gate, regroup, then strike out again," Steve continued. "We keep the monster where it is. Do not let the Wither get here, or it will be too late. We know arrows and dynamite aren't going to stop that thing. We'll have to figure out something."

Guards were eyeing them and listening with fear.

"A Wither can be easily defeated," one of the guards said. "But this isn't a normal Wither."

Steve didn't know whether to tell him the truth or not. To tell the people around them that he didn't know how to defeat the monster would probably just cause panic.

"This one can be too," Steve said, "though it's not so simple."

"So, tell us simply," another said.

"The Wither will be defeated," Steve shouted.

He turned and walked with Sam and the soldiers back to the Great Keep.

They reached the doors before too long, and Sam and Steve ascended the steps to the council chamber.

"A Super Wither, you say?" the king said.

"Yes," Steve responded. "It is worse than any mob that we've ever known, worse than even the Ender dragon. And it is thirty times what the regular Wither Bosses are."

"What if we trapped it there?" the Lord of the Armies asked. "What if we kept the monster there and never let the thing leave. There's no way to and from that world without a portal. We could clear the mines and leave that red waste to the creature."

"I hope you are right," Steve said.

"And if he is not, how do you plan to defeat it?" The king asked.

Steve thought for a moment as the air remained silent. Sam looked at him, and Steve could tell he had no idea either..

"When will the people reach North's End?"

"About two days," the Lord Governor said.

"Fortify Golden Gate with as much dynamite and soldiers as possible," Steve answered, hoping he knew what he was doing. "If the Wither gets out, it'll be drawn to a highly populated area. So, it will attack here first. Once we catch sight of it, send the people north, and then we defeat the mob here. And be ready for this world's mobs to attack. It seems whoever created the Wither is calling them to fight. The borderlands are proof of that."

The king thought for a moment.

"Alright," he said. "Recall the people."

The Lord Governor looked at Steve.

"I hope you're right," he said, and rose to leave.

Within moments, a wall of dynamite was built outside the

fortifications of the city. Archers lined the parapets, and miners were sent to harvest Netherite and trade with piglins for the material to strengthen the city. If they were attacked by the Wither, they would just regroup at the city and go to mine elsewhere.

Steve watched from one of the government buildings near the Keep.

The population began returning an hour later, with twice the number of people who had left, for they also included the population of many towns and farms near the city.

Steve watched them file through the gate with dread, hoping he wasn't dooming them all to a life of running and fear.

"You were always the brightest of colonizers," his father said.

He turned to see him.

"Father."

Steve's father smiled.

"Steve, you were able to solve the Academy's greatest problem, how to maintain the order and happiness of people while advancing. Where there is a city, there is chance for bad souls to flourish and affect others. But you found out how to keep that from happening yet still maintain the city. To remain true to who we are, living things of this world, and no more. No one else could truly understand that we are anchored to this planet, to this land, that to move away completely is mistaken. You can solve this too. You can solve this too, and that knowledge of how society ought to function will help us. This world is more a part of us than we could say. We must not lose it. You can do this."

Steve looked at him, heavy with responsibility, but grateful for the support.

"Father, the person who built the Wither told me that the world has strayed from the path set by the gods."

Steve's father's face grew serious.

"He said that that the gods created us without free will, but they trusted us after a while to be wise. Yet once they allowed us the freedom, we erred."

His father eyed him, thinking.

"That is a mere legend. There is some truth to it, but he lies."

Steve nodded.

"I thought so."

He turned to the banister.

Then he remembered something.

"Is Herobrine a legend too? I never bothered to look."

"Herobrine was named the Hidden by elder folk. Some accounts say he was first seen a hundred years ago, others that he helped win the war with the Withers. None of them can be confirmed or disproved. It is true he is real, and that he is different from most, but what the accounts say of him should be considered with a grain of salt. They don't all make sense and are not consistent. It is true, there is much about this world we don't understand, but what we do know is that everything can be explained. So we may trust that there is a reason for Herobrine being here."

Steve considered.

He nodded.

"I'm going to find him."

Chapter 11: A Friend

"You will have to be careful. Nothing is certain about him," his father said.

"I understand. He called himself a friend, and said he prayed we never understood what was happening."

"Perhaps he meant he never wanted us to go through what we are about to."

Steve frowned.

"You think he's a friend."

"It's a possibility, but he could also be an enemy."

"I once thought he could be a friend, till I saw him with the guy who built and unleashed the Wither."

"There is more to anyone than you can tell from just seeing them without understanding. Talk with him, and you may learn the truth."

"I'll go with Sam."

Steve turned and started descending the spiraling steps that joined the main street, then crossed to the Great Keep, where Sam was preparing for the fight.

He knocked at the door.

"It's Steve," he said.

"What is it?"

Steve walked through and closed the door.

"I'm going back there," he said. "I've got to find Herobrine."

Sam's face was mad.

"Are you crazy? Going back there now is stupid, and we know Herobrine's an enemy. He works with that hooded guy."

"Does he?" Steve said. "Why would the elders write legends where he's a hero if he isn't. Perhaps he's an anti-hero."

"What's your goal?"

"If he's a friend, he will help."

"And what if he isn't?"

"Then we'll defeat him too."

Sam thought for a while.

"Fine," he said. "But if Herobrine is bad, I ain't sparing him."

Steve nodded.

"I got my weapons and supplies. We can leave now," Sam said.

"We'll go back to the abandoned city first," Steve said, and they left.

The portal was now amidst a construction site, where soldiers were setting up the dynamite and preparing the archers' stations at the merlons. Netherite arrows were beginning to be crafted, along with Netherite blades, and were entrusted to only the best fighters.

Steve and Sam stepped through the portal and returned to the abandoned city.

At once, they caught sight of the Wither, floating amidst the red sky, its red eyes casting beams of light that scoured the ground.

Steve and Sam darted away from one just as it swept past the portal.

"Stay out of the light," Steve said. "And keep quiet. We'll head back to the lair first."

Steve walked on, crouched, with Sam following.

Beams of red light scoured the ground, and Steve and Sam ran to an obsidian heap just as the beams reached it.

They shined past the corners of the obsidian, missing them by a hair's breadth.

Steve let out a breath of relief when the beams moved away.

He left the safety of the heap and walked on, toward the giant mob.

It shrieked, all of a sudden, and Sam was standing beside him, transfixed, with red light shining on his armor.

"Sam!" Steve said, as a pair of the Wither's jaws launched a round of fire at him.

Sam ran out of the light and followed Steve as the fire crashed and went off, carving out a crater.

The beams of light were scurrying, looking for the two of them, as Steve and Sam ran, darting here, almost falling there, staying out of the light.

The wither shrieked again, but none of its eyes found them as they hid at the corner of an obsidian hill.

Steve looked out from where they were hiding.

The Wither was searching the ground frantically, like some mad creature. And then it began to move, gliding over to where they were hiding.

"Move," Steve said, and they ran from the corner, towards another area of the hill.

They saw the beams break over the hill, scouring the ground ahead.

Then they turned away, and there was silence once more.

A minute went by before Steve and Sam got up to see.

He walked to the corner of the hill and saw the wither floating nearby, its eyes searching the ground and hill. It seemed to have forgotten them.

Then a piglin wandered out of the shadows, and was caught by one of the eyes. The wither did nothing.

"This thing is evil," Steve said. "We can tell what is by how it treats the mobs. Piglins are clearly bad."

Steve and Sam ran out from the safety of the hill opposite where they had first sought refuge, and bolted for the lair where Herobrine was last seen.

They avoided the Wither's eyes. Luckily, there were not many mobs around to see them, so they went away without being noticed.

They reached the ruins of the towers a half hour later. The obsidian curtain was still there, cratered here and there, but the towers were almost demolished. Only one remained, its second half suspended by the cliff.

Steve and Sam ran towards it and began the climb. When they reached the gap, they bridged the way with some stone, and then ascended to the cliff where they had first run from the wither.

There was the fog again, but no sign of anything else.

When they reached the clearing, there was no one there.

Then Herobrine appeared beside him.

Sam was so startled he almost fell, and Steve looked at him, unable to say anything.

"I am a friend," Herobrine said. "I said I wished you would never understand because I wished you would never
have to. The legends tell it true. I fought with your people."

Steve looked at him, still unable to say anything.

"You're not one of us?" He managed.

"No. I am not of this world. But I am here to help you. I have remained hidden and worked secretly to protect you from enemies you cannot hope to fight. This time, I had to feign joining the enemy."

"So, you're working to defeat them?"

"Yes, the Wither and its creator."

Chapter 12: The Battle

"Nothing like this has happened before," Sam said. "You're certain we can make it through?"

"If we act wisely," Herobrine said.

Steve looked at him.

"We've got to trust him," he said. "He's our only chance. Why did you loose those arrows at me?"

"Because if I didn't, the One's Disciple would have believed it odd. And you were wearing armor. They would not have hurt you. And if you weren't, I trusted you would get out before you suffered too much damage."

"Thoughtful," Steve said. "Alright, so what do we do?"

"You're already doing it. Head back to Golden Gate. The city must be ready."

With that, Herobrine disappeared.

"You really think we can trust him?" Sam said.

"We have no choice."

The two headed back for the portal. When they stepped through, they found the city being fortified for the attack. Most of the preparations were complete.

Hills of dynamite rose up from the ground, threatening to detonate near the beast.

They would have to attack the computer block to break it all down, though that block was guarded by the strongest material of the earth.

Sam and Steve strode to the steps and ascended to the parapets.

From there, amongst the soldiers, they could see the fields beyond, the farms a few hundred blocks away, the trees, and the greenery, everything that was good about the world.

And the Wither would take it all if they did not stop it.

"The Wither will reach this world," Steve said to the soldiers. "The fight will be unlike any the world has seen, not even like those of the ancestors, when they saved the realm from the army of withers that had formed to occupy the world. This is our chance to be heroes! Our names will forever be remembered as those who guarded the world from darkness. You. What is your name?"

He was pointing at one of the guards.

"Me, sir? I'm Jon."

"Jon, by the time this battle's over, you could be a hero. Any of you can be. None of us truly die. But our lives are useless if we spend the rest of them running from this monster. We defeat the Wither here, we rebuild, and we live, not just survive."

"Yah!" The soldiers cheered.

He turned to Sam, who was clapping.

"Careful," he said, "get too popular and they may start calling for you to be mayor."

Steve laughed.

"Oh, friend, what a blessing that would be."

Sam laughed, but then his face changed, and he looked at Steve with a serious expression.

By nightfall, Steve was walking by the shield of dynamite.

He could hear chatter from the city and the parapets, where the men were calming their nerves.

Herobrine appeared.

"Steve," he said. "The Disciple knows I'm not his ally. It

doesn't matter now. I'm here to help. Your fortifications are rudimentary, but that makes no matter."

"Hey!"

"Sorry, but I will add to them. The Wither will be here soon. The Disciple is building a portal capable of teleporting it. Get to the battlements."

Steve nodded, and turned to head back to the city. Herobrine was already there when he reached the crenellations, standing amongst the soldiers.

The people of Golden Gate eyed him with weary eyes, silent.

"He's a friend," Steve told them. "He's here to help. He's never harmed us before, you know?"

"True," Jon said.

"Thank you," Herobrine said, and turned to the merlon.

One by one the stone blocks that formed the parapets, the walkway, and the wall transformed to Netherite blocks.

Then the buildings of the city.

Even the Keep and the tower were transformed.

When all the city had been turned to Netherite, the soldiers eyed Herobrine with awe.

"You're one of the Ancient Builders, aren't you?" Steve said. "The Builders today have a part of that magic left. That's how they build such grand structures."

Herobrine nodded.

"I was the first Builder. But I was cursed to a life of darkness. I tried to build something that all the laws of nature said could not be built. A portal to another world. The planet is part of this system, orbiting the same sun, with the right conditions for life. This world has been threatened by different monsters for millennia. I thought that this other world be safe, and thought I might build a Golden Gate so that all the people of this world might travel to that one. But nature refused, and for my crime, sentenced me to an eternity of making things right, while all would see me as evil. I have spent a thousand years staying away from you all, helping where possible. I never talked before because I would be misunderstood. Now, the gods have seen fit to end my sentence if I help to defeat this. Though, it is necessary as well. And now I'm here to help, but for the last time."

"What?" Steve said.

"The universe said the only way I would be allowed peace is if I saved the world from its greatest threat, the threat that would not threaten for a thousand years. It's here now. And once we defeat the threat, I will be released, for I have lived centuries past my time. None of us live forever, just a few thousand years."

Steve looked at him sadly.

"You can't leave," he said. "You're the best of us."

Herobrine smiled.

"I am of a different time, a different world. New heroes should be allowed a chance to stand, heroes such as all of you."

Steve nodded.

"Then you're a greater friend than I thought."

Then they heard a noise like the sound of lightning.

Light lashed the dynamite and Netherite defenses as the portal formed.

Steve turned towards it.

The purple Golden Gate was there, shifting. It was ten times as big as a regular portal. It was not natural.

The soldiers watched silently, bows trained.

Steve kept watch as well.

They saw a round of fire fly from the portal, striking the ground near one of the dynamite hills.

A crater erupted beside the pile, luckily not triggering the TNT.

And then the creature appeared.

One by one its heads emerged from the portal, launching fire. The ground was dotted with craters before long.

"Loose!" Steve said.

The archers let fly their arrows. They struck the creature, and the might of a thousand arrows saw the wither blink red.

And then they saw the Disciple, walking alongside the Wither as the Netherite blocks that shielded the computer emerged.

"Launch at that man!" the Lord of the Armies said.

The archers loosed, but the arrows fell onto a shield that deflected them back.

An ominous laugh sounded.

"You are fools," the Disciple said. "You too as well, Herobrine. You all will fall, and the One will triumph. The age of the mobs is here!"

"Herobrine!" Steve said.

Herobrine launched a round of flame, sending it hurtling towards the dynamite pile nearest the Wither.

The TNT began to go off. The Wither shrieked, dodging it, but a few of the Wither heads broke off, and disappeared as puffs of smoke.

Then the rest rained fire while the dynamite blocks dotted the craters with bigger craters.

"Get him to the dynamite wall before he targets the thing himself!"

Rounds of fire began racing toward them. The fire soared past the dynamite, and struck the merlons.

A part of the parapet disappeared, and a number of the soldiers, but they respawned at the steps and raced back up as other rounds of fire hit the battlements.

Herobrine launched a line of fire at the Wither. But the monster suffered no wounds as it glided forward, its red eyes searching, beams of light scouring the ground, fire racing from it.

Herobrine fashioned Netherite walls where the fire was racing toward the dynamite.

The Netherite stones remained strong, holding back the flames.

Herobrine lit up another one of the dynamite hills as a flight of arrows raced from the crenelations.

The dynamite broke off chunks of the Wither, while the arrows affected its health.

The Disciple was standing near the Wither, and he launched a block of lava at the wall.

Herobrine conjured water and doused the flames, letting the block of obsidian crash before the Netherite blocks.

The Wither was heading for the city. The dynamite blocks were all lit up now, and shrill shrieks split the air.

Herobrine launched rounds of fire at the Netherite shielding the computer. The shell broke away before long, but the Disciple just replaced it a moment later.

Steve knew he would have to get rid of the computer himself.

He turned and headed for the steps. Sam turned to follow.

Silently, they reached the gate, where the soldiers were standing ready to fight the Wither.

Steve opened the oak door and then the iron gate.

"Steve," Sam said. "The chances of getting through are not high."

"I know," Steve said. "But there's a chance."

He left the city. Sam followed as rounds of fire raced to strike Netherite blocks. The ground was a great crater, with staggering blocks of earth leading from the surface.

Steve ran towards it, then began to go around.

He and Sam forded the rift where only three blocks of earth had broken off. They ran toward the Wither, all its eyes staring at the city as fire raced toward the Netherite shields that Herobrine crafted.

Arrows were falling on the creature and the Disciple was shouting, launching fire and lava at the city. He seemed to not notice Sam and Steve as they ran towards the Wither.

Steve began building a stone ladder and climbed up to the Wither.

None of its eyes saw him, and he leapt high. As soon as he landed, the Wither shrieked and lurched, trying to throw him off. The fire barrage ended and its heads were turning, trying to find him and Sam as he landed on the ground.

Sam started striking the soul sand blocks while Steve headed for the Netherite shield.

Arrow-fire had stopped as well. The field was burning, and the battle was now between two heroes and the Wither.

As Steve moved towards the Netherite shield, a round of fire raced toward him.

He dodged it, and it flew away, but then another hurtled towards him, launched by the Disciple.

Steve dodged this one as well and kept walking towards the shield as the Wither lurched and shrieked, unable to see him.

He reached the shield before long.

Ignoring the fire that raced past him, he struck the Netherite.

Sam was mining the soul sand blocks, but the Disciple just replaced them.

Steve managed to mine the first Netherite block a few moments later.

He used it to strike the computer, but the computer suffered no damage, and the shield reformed.

Steve saw that the Disciple was launching a round of fire at him. He turned and ran.

"Sam!" He shouted.

He leapt away from the Wither and fell to the ground. Sam landed a moment later, and started running towards him.

And now the Wither saw them. It launched a hail of fire, setting the ground alight.

Herobrine launched fire at the creature again, and once they spotted Sam and Steve, the archers loosed another round of arrows at the Wither.

Sam and Steve ran back towards the city.

The soldiers greeted them with cheers as they ran back up to the battlements.

"The computer is guarded," Steve said.

"Then it is guarded by some sort of potion, or a spell. We'll have to eliminate the Disciple first, before we can truly deal with the Wither. Focus all your weapons on him," Herobrine said.

The soldiers began directing their arrows toward the Disciple while Herobrine launched fire at him. He deflected each one. The Wither was still being hurt by the arrows, and it was still firing at the city.

At that moment, skeletons, withers, ghouls, ghasts, piglins, zoglins, and other mobs began filing out of the portal.

"You're kidding," Sam said, angry.

Steve equipped his bow.

Creepers began emerging from the trees, heading for the city. It was as if all darkness was being summoned.

"Target the mobs! If they reach the city, there's no stopping the Wither!"

Steve loosed an arrow at a creeper. The mob disappeared as smoke as Sam loosed an arrow and the archers targeted the rest, while Herobrine kept firing at the Wither.

Steve slew a skeleton as the ghasts began firing at the city. Herobrine crafted Netherite shields to guard the city and the dynamite. Steve loosed an arrow at a piglin and the mob disappeared.

Arrows from the skeletons raced up the walls, but missed, and the archers cut the skeletons down before too long.

Steve loosed another arrow, and hit a zoglin. He loosed another, then another, and the thing was gone.

Then he aimed at a wither marching along with the red-eyed Supreme Wither. He fired two arrows, and the smaller wither fell.

The Supreme Wither had lost a few of its heads, but not enough to make a difference, and more mobs were pouring through the portal and out of the trees.

"Herobrine! Target them with dynamite!"

Herobrine placed dynamite blocks amidst the mobs and set them alight.

The TNT tore new craters and eliminated many of the mobs. A trench formed before the Wither, and the mobs fell there.

Any that clambered out were struck by arrows.

The Disciple walked forward, eyeing the battlements with rage.

Then he launched fire at them. Herobrine tried to build shields, but the fires went around and soared past the crenellations.

They spread amidst the streets. The Netherite buildings were safe, but the fields of harvested farms were set alight and the yard where soldiers trained began to burn.

The Disciple launched another fire.

It went around Herobrine's shields and struck the city.

"Target him," Steve said.

Flights of arrows and rounds of fire from Herobrine were directed at the Disciple. They flew through the chunks of floating Netherite that Herobrine had crafted to shield everyone from the fire.

But the Disciple deflected them all.

They kept up the attack, but the Wither launched fire at them. Herobrine built shields while they loosed flights of arrows and Herobrine launched flame.

Steve kept targeting his arrows.

Then the Wither shrieked and fired at the city, all one hundred rounds racing to a point at the dynamite wall.

Herobrine tried to conjure a Netherite shield, but the fire broke through and struck the dynamite.

The explosion shattered the wall, cracked the earth, and a trench sprouted from the northern to the western gate.

Steve awoke by one of the cobblestone streets. He had on a simple shirt and trousers, but no armor or weapons.

Many more like him were standing with him, with no armor left.

Steve looked up and saw the great gap where a large section of the wall had been. Their gear floated there, and the Wither was beyond.

Fire arced across the sky and fell on the city. The Netherite shells were failing, and fires were erupting.

"Regain your posts!" Steve shouted.

He ran forward to the steps. The steps were still there, and so was his stuff. He gathered everything, donned his armor, and raced up as a round of fire soared past the battlements.

The other soldiers arrived as well, with Sam.

Herobrine was still there, firing at the creature.

He was targeting the computer's Netherite shield.

The Wither shrieked and lurched, trying to defend its brain, but Herobrine launched the fire around it. He was able to strike despite the Wither's efforts to keep the computer safe.

The Netherite shell disappeared and then hit the computer block.

A blinding light lashed the world and Steve closed his eyes.

When he opened them, the Wither was still there, and it had healed.

Herobrine eyed the monster with rage. Then he turned his arms toward the Disciple, and fired.

The Disciple's defense weakened, and it was gone a moment later.

Next, the fire struck him, and the Disciple disappeared with a blinding light.

"He's gone," Herobrine said.

The soldiers cheered.

"The fight's not over," Steve said. "The creature's mind is gone, but the Wither's brain still lives. As long as the brain continues, it will not fall. Though the creature's control is gone now, which will make our task that much easier. We have to get rid of that computer."

"Only you can do that," Herobrine said. "The computer is built to heal. And only the power of the gods can stop it. You are no god, and I am not. But you can call upon them."

"Why can't you?"

"I'm guilty of a crime."

Steve eyed him solemnly.

"Okay," he said. "But I need your help to keep the Wither distracted while I get to the computer."

Herobrine nodded.

"Sam, Jon, with me."

He turned and descended the wall to the gate. The city was still burning, and the Wither was still launching fire at the streets.

Herobrine fired back.

The Wither shrieked and fired at him, but they dealt no damage. Herobrine's fires chipped away the soul sand and some of the fire dispensers, as the three soldiers ran toward it.

They leapt small craters, went around greater ones, and darted past fields of fire.

They reached the shadow of the creature and ran for the steps Steve had built earlier to reach the thing. It was still there, and they could leap the distance. So, they climbed the stone steps and launched.

They landed and the Wither shrieked, trying to throw them off.

Steve looked and saw that the Netherite shell was already missing a block where Herobrine had struck it, but the computer was still there.

He ran towards it.

Jon and Sam mined at the Wither as Steve stood before the computer.

Herobrine was striking the Wither's heads with fire, while it fired back.

"Gods," Steve said. "The gods who lent the Builders power to craft this world, the gods who allowed us eternal life, ability, and intelligence, I call upon you for the power to save my people, members of the universe. I will use your power justly, I will defend this world, and for that, I ask, free Herobrine of his sentence. Let him live freely, to build as a Builder, and not hide from time, to live as he would have before his crime."

But Steve didn't really believe that Herobrine had committed a crime by trying to help the people.

He also knew that by breaking the computer, he might lose all his memory because of the energy wave that would fly out.

The wind gusted, and Steve could hear it, despite the battle.

The Wither still rebuilt the shell, and piled more Netherite, soul sand, and diamond around it.

Steve staggered back as the Wither grew.

"This thing doesn't need the Disciple!" Steve said.

Sam and Jon eyed the site where the computer was. More blocks were fortifying it, and it was still launching fire at the city.

Steve mined the blocks before the Wither could replace them and went to stand amidst the gap.

Then he mined another space, and walked there, just as the

first one sealed off with obsidian.

The chamber was strangely illuminated, and he could feel the movement of the Wither as it fired at the city and fortified its computer.

He could not hear Sam or Jon, or the sound of the rounds of fire crashing, or Herobrine's fires reaching the Wither.

The narrow space was illuminated by crystal lights. They shifted from color to color, and Steve started mining.

The beast lurched and he leapt through the gap as the Wither sealed it off.

He mined again, and went ahead.

Ten times he did this before he found the Netherite shell.

He did not have the time to mine the two blocks for him to get through. He was thinking about what to do when Sam appeared beside him, and the gap sealed.

"Figured out how you did it," Sam said. "Easy."

Steve laughed.

"Help me get through this. The computer block is not far."

They both mined the Netherite and darted through.

They mined through the second block, and then the third.

Sam mined a spot for him to stand.

Here, there was no area for the Wither to place another defense. They were standing where the last space was, and even darkness could not bend the laws of the world.

He could see the computer, its buttons glowing. Green and red lights flickered. They looked like firing neurons.

Steve and Sam equipped their enchanted swords.

"We'll be heroes," Sam said.

"No doubt. Three, two, one."

The two struck the computer block.

They heard the Wither shriek and struck again.

Two more and the computer was gone.

At once, they felt like they were falling, and they heard a last sorrowful shriek as the power left the Wither and the mob crashed.

The blocks around them disappeared into clouds of smoke, and Steve and Sam looked to see that the Wither was gone.

Steve almost couldn't believe it. He could recognize Sam in front of him, they had defeated the monster, and they had saved the world.

They heard cheering, and turned to see the soldiers shouting from the battlements. Herobrine stood amongst them, silent as he usually was, but Steve could sense his peace mixed with sorrow.

"The Wither's gone," Sam said.

Steve nodded.

"The world is saved!" Jon shouted.

"And you're both heroes!" Steve declared.

Jon was smiling, and Sam too. Steve rose.

The fields of fire, cratered earth, and the broken city were no longer sightings that caused despair, but were
testimonies to the will and strength of people.

Together, they walked back to the city, laughing and talking.

The clamor of cheering grew louder as they reached Golden Gate.

Most of the fires were being doused and the city rang with shouts of joy.

"Steve!" They chanted. "Steve!"

Steve looked at them all.

Many were people he did not know, but he found he cared for them anyway. His father had told him that that was what made a good leader, when someone cared for the good of those he didn't even know, so that when he might govern, he looked out for all.

Herobrine appeared beside him.

"Steve," he said. "You have defeated the Wither, and you have set me free. I thank you."

"I did not set you free according to that meaning," Steve told him. "The gods granted me your life as it would have been if I slew the beast. You will live for as long as you would have now, free to build, free to craft, and free to be among us."

Herobrine looked at him with surprise.

"Thank you, Steve."

"There is one last thing I require your help with. I need to find out who the One is. The Disciple is probably just one of his cronies, and this attack is just one that failed. Will there be another? How do we defend it? We'll talk later."

Chapter 13: The Dark One

That night, fireworks lit up the night sky.

The Builders rebuilt the city fortifications and people rebuilt their homes. People were cheering and laughing, and Herobrine reformed the ground and closed the portal the Disciple had crafted to let the Wither out.

Food and drink crowded the trestle tables of the great hall, and the people were happy.

Jon and Sam and Steve were proclaimed as heroes, but soon after, Steve found himself leaving the noise and laughter for the relative quiet of the outside.

Herobrine was there, watching the fields from the battlements.

Steve walked up to him.

"The One is an ancient god," Herobrine told him, "older than the planet, older than time. He was one of the gods, and worked alongside them to build the cosmos, fighting threats we could never hope to combat. When this planet was crafted, he requested that he might form an army here, an army of the gods armed with the power of the gods, to ensure that their worship was secure, and that no false gods were conjured by their subjects.

"All the gods rebuked him, and they cast him out, locking his powers away. He swore vengeance, and turned to the dark side, where the powers are greater because they are fouler. And now he has returned. A war of the gods is being fought, and the One is supported by the dark, and seeks to ensure its worship."

Steve looked at him, horrified.

"So the One sent the Disciple and this monster."

Herobrine nodded.

"How are we supposed to fight a god?"

"You can only fight him by denying him a chance to wield his powers. The gods are powerful, but they are limited by the necessity to physically be where they wish to affect. They cannot affect anywhere remotely. Which means the One is somewhere here. And the gods are not as superior as they think. Leave no area abandoned. Colonize the world. Colonize the Nether. I believe it is time for that."

Steve looked at him.

"The Nether could be colonized, though it's no easy task."

"When was anything easy?" Herobrine said. "There's is no way to slay a god. The gods are immortal. But you can deny them power. The One will not have power here if there is nowhere for him to wield it from. The Nether, as it is, would be his workplace, but the colonies there shall be armed with defenses and weapons to fight him. I shall see to that."

Steve thought.

"Okay," he said. "But I'm not the one you gotta convince. You'll have to speak to the council."

"I will."

"Then we'll start by colonizing the Nether," Steve said. "This world is not nearly as dangerous, so it would be better to handle that one first."

"Wise."

Dawn arrived to see the people of Golden Gate returned to work. They had spent the last few hours of the night asleep, so now they were running their shops and stalls again. Farmers were planting new crops, and life had returned to normal, as if the Wither had never attacked.

Herobrine and Steve stood before the council. All mayors had also been gathered, and they sat amongst them.

"You want to colonize the Nether?" The king asked.

"It sounds crazy, but I don't think it is," Steve said. "The One is dangerous, and he will most likely be there. But he cannot affect us if we are there to stop him. We can never slay him, but perhaps when he finds there is nowhere for him to strike from, he will leave. And we'll colonize the rest of this green earth to, to rid us of all the mobs that roam the uncultivated lands."

The council considered him.

"What does your friend Herobrine think?" The king asked.

"It was his idea. And he's all of our friend. He saved us, and is promising to save this world from anything else like that Wither and an evil god."

The king looked at Herobrine.

"You're no villain, I can see that. Though you are strange. Steve told me you're one of the Ancient Builders. I can see that's true. You've helped us, and with more than just the Wither. You've actually helped many more times. I suppose the gunship was to be used to fight the Wither?"

"Yes. But you didn't need it."

"Well, thanks for that, and your plan is approved. The gunship will be used to aid the colonization."

"Thank you," Steve said. "This will work. Could you call for an audience?"

The king nodded.

"You shall speak from the balcony of the keep."

Herobrine and Steve left the council chamber.

"That was not as difficult as I believed it would be," Steve said.

"When the path is right, no one can disagree without lying to themselves."

Steve pondered those words for a moment.

Sam joined them then.

"I'll be helping," he said.

Steve smiled.

They headed to the balcony of the keep.

A moment later, the king and the council and the mayors arrived.

They heard a great trumpet sounding, and a few moments later, the people turned to hear.

The king gestured for Steve to speak.

"People of Golden Gate!" Steve shouted. "It has been decreed that this world and the Nether will be colonized. That Wither was just one of many things that will attack us if we do not complete this. The one who sent the Wither is called the One. He is a terrible god. The Nether is where he is. And we can clearly fight whatever he sends to attack us, but if we were to colonize the Nether, there'd be nowhere for him to create more threats. And then he will leave. We will colonize this world too. We'll be free of all the mobs then."

The people looked at him, and they shouted agreement, but one voice spoke louder than the others.

"The Nether is dangerous! How are we supposed to colonize there without being attacked?"

"Herobrine built us a gunship! It will be used to
defend each colony as its being built. And all our armies will be sent as well. We have no threats here. The real ones are there!'"

That settled it.

The Builders boarded trains and went through the portals. Columns of soldiers marched through, and people were signing up to help.

The first colony, Steve decided, would be the abandoned one. It was closest to the Disciple's lair, and one that should've been completed long ago.

Colonizers were sent to the mines to build towns.

Steve and Jon and Sam walked through the portal to the abandoned colony.

The builders were already beginning to complete the fortifications and the soldiers were standing guard. Herobrine was there, watching the Builders. The keep was completed, and torches lit. The farms were readied with soil and sand transported from Golden Gate, and the cellars were lit with torches and cleared of mobs.

A few hours later, the city was complete, as it was supposed to be, but Steve had plans for new buildings.

"Jon," he said, when the city was beginning to be populated, "I would like you to be mayor of this town. You are not a soldier anymore. I will consult the council, but I'm sure you'll be awarded this."

Jon smiled happily.

"It would be an honor, Steve. Thank you."

By day's end, Jon was mayor of the colony, and a total of five more colonies had been set up since Steve's speech.

As of yet, there had been no attacks. The colony at North-North-West Mine was already built, and the gunship was being sent to Far West. An hour later, it went to where Steve had set up his house when he first decided to chase Herobrine.

Steve decided he would establish that colony, and so he gathered Builders and soldiers and left promptly. He got back to Golden Gate by portal, then walked to Beaconlight.

Sean was there waiting, and Steve fed him again.

Beaconlight was faring well. All the people had returned. They had left for Golden Gate before, along the way to North's End when the world was threatened by a Wither. Now that things were safe, the farms were being harvested again and talk could be heard from the marketplace.

He walked to the portal and stepped through, as the soldiers and Builders followed.

His house was still there, as well as the soul torches.

They walked down to it.

"This house will be the keep of the city. Build as you would."

The Builders started crafting houses, armories, and the ring of torches. The soldiers kept watch on the horizon the gunship looming above. The city formed before his eyes. Red earth was replaced with cobble roads and the house was transformed to a Netherite and stone keep, with a tower that allowed one to see for miles.

Before the hour was gone, the city had been built.

Steve turned to head back to Beaconlight.

"A new city has been established, just beyond this Golden Gate," he said. "I'm sure you have all heard the news by now. I'm calling for those who would be willing to populate this city. Live there as colonizers, as settlers of a new world. Keep golden armor with you, for piglins don't attack unless you wear golden armor, and we do not seek to kill anyone. But be armed, anyway. If any of you refuse to do this, you are doing no wrong."

Silence went by for a minute.

"I will go," an old man said. "Me and my enchanted sword. Finally managed to craft this yesterday."

Steve nodded.

"I as well," another said, "with my family."

Two young lads, the man's wife, and an older man stepped forward.

"And me," another said.

Before long, most of the yard had signed up to go to the new city.

They marched through the portal happily with their things, and beheld streets illuminated by lanterns and the ring of torches, as well as the warped fungi trees that the Builders had planted. The Nether no longer seemed so frightening.

New Beaconlight, Steve named the town, and he found that the fungi he'd planted a few days ago was growing nicely.

Then the soldiers and Builders were called to another sector of the Nether to build another town there.

The colonization was going well.

So far, nothing had attacked them. It seemed evil had diminished since they defeated the Disciple. But the One was still here. Steve trusted that this would send him away, but this world could not be colonized within just a few days. It would be years before all this land was city and town, before all the Nether Fortresses were demolished, and the land was safe. Till then, the One could still harbor his projects here, and plot. He was immortal. He couldn't be slain. Steve decided he would have to send him away somehow.

Magic and the tales of the gods were things Steve had never really paid any attention to. However, each city had its scholars, and Golden Gate housed the most. He would be able to find his answers there.

So, he headed back to the city.

The Street of Scholars was flanked by great stone buildings, all of them libraries. They housed thousands of accounts written by historians, commoners, and any who wielded a quill.

He walked through the door of the first one to his right.

The hall was dark, except for the burning of a few torches. Shelves of books formed aisles along the hall, and there were stairs going up to more shelves.

Steve found the librarian sitting by one of the torches, his old eyes squinting.

"Sir," he said, "where might I find a book about the gods. About the One, perhaps?"

The old man almost looked like he wasn't moving.

"Fifth floor, aisle eight, column three," he muttered. "Theology: The Gods and Godly Matters."

Steve nodded and turned to head to the stairs.

He climbed, seeing nothing but torches and books.

There were a few people reading amidst the silence of the library, and soon Steve reached the fifth floor.

The book was just where he had been told.

<u>Theology: The Gods and Godly Matters</u>

He retrieved the book and headed to a table illuminated by a torch.

He scoured the table of contents and flipped to the chapter about the six gods. There was the Builder, who crafted the cosmos, the Thinker, who created life, the Mother, who granted immortality to the people, the Warrior, who crafted the first weapons that ancient people used, the Light One, and the Dark One. Each god had pages, but the Dark One populated just half a page.

'Shunned,' it read, 'he was the brother of the Light One, trusted with the responsibilities too dark for the other gods to handle. The worlds were peaceful, but the peace of the world could only be kept by fighting otherworldly threats. He was the warrior of the gods. But his powers grew dark, and his wars diminished what light he was blessed with. Then there were some peoples who created new religions. He saw them as heretics and their gods as false, while the other gods recognized that the people had a right to believe. The Dark One thought he could end heresy by deploying godly armies to defeat their worship. He was cast out, the wars ended, evil proceeded unchecked, and the mobs of the world were born.' That was all the account would tell him.

He tried searching for anything more. But there wasn't anything else to find.

So, he left the library. It was dark by then, and Herobrine was standing outside.

"The gods are real," Steve told him. "I spoke to them. That's why you're here now. If I can speak to them again, I could rid us of the Dark One. The colonization will take too long. The Dark One will have the chance to strike again."

Herobrine considered his words before responding.

"The gods did not create everything," he said. "For they were created by energy, and the will of the universe. And one of the laws that the cosmos set was that a god may never slay another god. It was a safeguard to ensure that those powers would always rule jointly. Even those who might have been corrupted would find they had no choice but to work with the other gods. So the rest of them cannot slay the Dark
One, and casting him out was all they could do."

"So, I can talk to the cosmos?" Steve asked.

"You can. But can you really? It takes a great deal of patience and effort to do so."

"Do you know how to?"

"No. But there have been those who can."

"And there are none now."

"Not as I know."

"How can I learn?"

"Just try. Be calm. It will hear you."

Steve returned to Beaconlight to ponder. Sean was there, and the city was alive.

He closed his eyes, and thought about how he had spoken with the gods, how he had agreed to defeat the computer, even though it could've erased his mind, if they freed Herobrine.

But those were the gods. And there was a greater power he'd never known about. How would he talk to something he'd never known was there, didn't truly recognize, and didn't know much about?

But he asked the question nonetheless.

"How do I defeat the Dark One?"

No answer greeted him but the sound of the city and Sean wandering about, his claws tapping the oaken boards.

Then Steve realized something.

He just knew that the Dark One was where the Wither had been released. He was there, planning some other attack, with Ender dragons.

Steve realized that there was no way he could have found that out himself. The thought had reached him as if it were the words of another, not the notions of his own mind. He realized the cosmos had replied.

Happy, wiser, and confident, he left his house and returned to New Beaconlight.

He went to the balcony of the keep.

The herald was there.

"Gather the people," he said.

The herald sounded the trumpet. At once, the people turned to listen to their mayor.

"The horrors of this world, and the Wither, were the work of the Dark One, the outcast god. The colonization of this world shall continue, and will rid us of those that wish to harm us, but the task will not be complete for years. So the Dark One must be defeated now before he can strike again. All soldiers, I call upon you, be ready to march for his lair where the Wither was released. I will call for the forces of Golden Gate and the other cities. We will defeat the Dark God, and then even the mobs already here won't have a leader to follow to war."

At once, the soldiers formed up beyond the ring of torches.

They would march.

Steve turned and headed back to the portal.

From Beaconlight, he ran to Golden Gate and rallied the

armies there. Mayor Jon arrived with his troops, Sam with his, and many more. Steve felt a pang of doubt strike him.

Was he leading these men to suffering, if the Dark One was there? They were immortal, and the Dark One was powerful. They could be condemned to fates of pain.

Steve disregarded the thought.

He would see the Dark One gone, and the world free of him. But the Dark One could not be killed. Steve decided he would have to talk with him, while fifty thousand soldiers fought whatever monsters he threw at them.

"Warriors of Golden Gate!" He shouted. "Warriors of all the world! You are called here because though we have survived the Wither, we have not survived the real threat. The Dark One hides, plotting to attack again. We all know the tale. He sought to snuff out other creeds by sending armies to secure the worship of the first gods. But the other gods judged him wrong, for he was not just. So he turned to the darkness, learning powers forbidden and ancient. And now he is here. He fashioned a monster that would have seen the blocks of this world reduced to smoke, and he will attack again if we do not defeat him now. But the Dark One cannot be slain. I must speak with him. Or I must call upon the energy of the cosmos to rid us of him forever. One of them will be done. I call upon you to aid me. There will be defenses that he will use to try to keep us away from him, but we must fight through those. If any of you do not wish to go, you may stay. No one will think you dishonorable or cowardly."

Silence prevailed.

No one seemed to wish to stay.

"Then we march now."

He turned and descended the steps to the cobble road and strode with his enchanted blade to the portal to Heroes' Realm, where Jon was now the mayor. The king and council watched him as he stood there, eyeing the Golden Gate.

"For the world," he said, and stepped through.

He appeared amidst the yard of Heroes' Realm's portal. Herobrine and the soldiers began marching through a moment later, and he walked ahead. Soon, they were all marching away from the city. They reached the broken towers a half hour later. The column had broken to formations of a hundred, and their strength could be seen from miles away. No mob attacked them as they marched.

Steve ordered the towers rebuilt, and then the army began marching up, reaching the top a few minutes later.

Steve walked ahead of them with the other mayors, as the army marched from the towers.

The fog was still there as they reached the other side. They saw that the space where the Wither had been was still devoid of anything.

Steve spotted the archway the Dark One had left through after the Wither was unleashed.

"Careful," Herobrine warned. "He means to trap you."

"I know," Steve said, and started walking down. The soldiers followed suit, and soon they were pouring through the arch.

They placed torches as they went to chase away the darkness.

Crystal lights shifted, like those Steve had found when he was mining toward the computer block.

A shriek echoed amidst the darkness and they turned to see two purple eyes racing toward them, its wings fluttering as it flew.

"An Ender dragon," Steve muttered.

Perched atop it was a man whose garb was black. His face was black as night, and his eyes glowed red.

The Dark One.

PLEASE LEAVE A REVIEW

As a new author, I would appreciate feedback from my readers. It will help Minecraft fans like you discover my stories. Please share what you love about this book here. Thank you very much.

All rights reserved.

No part of this publication may be copied, reproduced in any format, by any means, electronic or otherwise, without prior consent from the copyright owner and publisher of this book.

Disclaimer

This is a work of fiction. Names, characters, businesses, places, events and incidents are either the products of the author's imagination or used in fictitious manner. Any resemblance to actual persons, living or dead, or actual events is purely coincidental.

This unofficial Minecraft book is not authorized, endorsed or sponsored by Microsoft Corp., Mojang AB, Notch Development AB or any other person or entity owning or controlling the rights of the Minecraft name, trademark or copyrights. All characters, names, places and other aspects of the game described herein are trademarked and owned by their respective owners. Minecraft®/ /TM & ©2009-2016 Mojang/Notch.

Printed in the USA
CPSIA information can be obtained
at www.ICGtesting.com
LVHW022119200624
783564LV00013B/814